Superyachts

Superyachts
Luxury, Tranquility and Ecocide

Grégory Salle

Translated by Helen Morrison

polity

Originally published in French as *Superyachts. Luxe, calme et écocide*
© Éditions Amsterdam, 2021

This English edition © Polity Press, 2024

Polity Press
65 Bridge Street
Cambridge CB2 1UR, UK

Polity Press
111 River Street
Hoboken, NJ 07030, USA

ISBN-13: 978-1-5095-5994-7 (hardback)
ISBN-13: 978-1-5095-5995-4 (paperback)

A catalogue record for this book is available from the British Library.

Library of Congress Control Number: 2023938505

Typeset in 11 on 14pt Warnock Pro
by Cheshire Typesetting Ltd, Cuddington, Cheshire
Printed and bound in Great Britain by CPI Group (UK) Ltd, Croydon

The publisher has used its best endeavours to ensure that the URLs for external websites referred to in this book are correct and active at the time of going to press. However, the publisher has no responsibility for the websites and can make no guarantee that a site will remain live or that the content is or will remain appropriate.

Every effort has been made to trace all copyright holders, but if any have been overlooked the publisher will be pleased to include any necessary credits in any subsequent reprint or edition.

For further information on Polity, visit our website:
politybooks.com

Contents

Contents

Acknowledgements

My thanks first of all to the team at the Saint-Tropez Marine Observatory (now known as 'Services espaces maritimes de la communauté de communes du golfe de Saint-Tropez'), who opened my eyes to the issues associated with the Posidonia seagrass meadows and so, unintentionally, launched me in an unforeseen direction. I have the greatest admiration for the work done by the professionals at the observatory and I am very much aware that the role of an 'outsider' is incomparably more comfortable than that of the actor dealing with the day-to-day challenges of the terrain.

Thanks also to Allan, whose wise suggestions enriched the original manuscript, and to Eva and Anne-Laure for their meticulous work.

I am grateful to Helen for the English translation, to Susan for her work on the manuscript and to Elise for her assistance at Polity.

And a special thank you to Christiane and Roland, Isa and Nina.

Abbreviations & acronyms

AIS   Automatic identification system

ATTAC   Association pour la taxation des transactions financières et pour l'action citoyenne (Association for the Taxation of Financial Transactions and for Citizens' Action)

CEN   Conservatoire d'espaces naturels (Association for the Protection of Natural Areas)

DDTM   Direction départementale des territoires et de la mer (Local Department for Land and Sea)

DREAL   Direction régionale de l'environnement de l'aménagement et du logement (Regional Department for the Environment, Planning and Housing)

EU   European Union

GIS   Groupement d'intérêt scientifique (Scientific interest group)

HNWI   High Net Worth Individuals

ICOMIA   International Council of Marine Industry Associations

IFI   Impôt sur la fortune immobilière (Tax on real estate)

INSEE   Institut national de la statistique et études économiques (National Institute of Statistics and Economic Studies)

ISF   Impôt de solidarité sur la fortune (Wealth tax)

LSE   London School of Economics

MYBA   Mediterranean Yacht Broker Association (Worldwide Yachting Association)

OFCE   Observatoire français des conjonctures économiques (French Economic Observatory)

PACA   Provence-Alpes-Côte d'Azur

PFU   Prélèvement forfaitaire unique (≈ flat tax)

RNLI   Royal National Lifeboat Institution

SNSM   Société nationale de sauvetage en mer (≈ French National Lifeboat Company)

UHNWI   Ultra-High-Net-Worth-Individuals

UNESCO   United Nations Educational, Scientific and Cultural Organization

ZMEL   Zone de mouillage et d'équipement léger (Anchorage and light equipment zone – regulated maritime area)

Figure 1 Portofino © Domenico FaronePixabay

Preface to the English edition

'Social Space: to recognize the space in which one finds oneself, one must discover its limits' declared Max Horkheimer (1994, p. 76) in a note written in the 1920s. The statement is both simple and haunting. In its own way, the book you are about to read reflects this idea. Begun in 2019, it was based on the premise that however futile they may seem, 'superyachts' (a convenient name which is in itself a symbolic show of strength, in the same way that so-called 'smartphones' are not in fact as 'intelligent' as their name implies), provide valuable insight into a telling aspect of the world in which we live, in a way that goes beyond their innate extravagance. As I write this preface, two years after its publication in France in April 2021, a number of events or incidents have served to confirm this idea.

In the intervening period, what was referred to at the end of the book, in a half-joking way, has taken on a more serious turn. In the context of Western sanctions against Russian assets, following the military invasion of Ukraine, a number of luxury yachts belonging to figures (believed to be) close to the Kremlin have been frozen in various home ports, usually while undergoing refits. This explains why a vessel believed to belong – via a shell entity – to Vladimir Putin and ironically named *Graceful* (the Russian despot is also reputed to be the indirect owner of *Scheherazade*, estimated to be worth 700 million euros when seized by Italian authorities in May 2022), which had spent several months docked in the port of Hamburg undergoing a refit, abruptly but discreetly left the location shortly before Russian troops invaded Ukraine. In fact, an extraordinary game of hide and seek was being played out between Russian oligarchs and government authorities, assisted by an informal community tracking vessels via geo-localization sites and social-media networks – even *Forbes* magazine got involved! A considerable number of superyachts known or presumed to be owned by Russian billionaires sought refuge in the Maldives, in Montenegro, in the Seychelles or elsewhere, sometimes (illegally) cutting their automatic identification systems in order to avoid being detected. The inexhaustible charms of the offshore economy . . .

It is easy to see where the value of a punitive seizure of such vessels would lie, at a time when most great accumulations of wealth have been rendered invisible as a result of the financialization of capital, a phenomenon that increases incrementally the higher you go up the scale of wealth. Such a 'catch' is visible, tangible and concrete. The imposing physical presence of the intended target paradoxically gives it a powerful symbolic dimension. It is, however, a falsely impressive capture, not least because of the legal fragility of the process involved. Nor does it go far enough in the context of any serious attempt at regulation. As Gabriel Zucman (2015) points out, setting up a register of financial wealth would be necessary in order to be able to tax, or perhaps freeze, the movable and immovable assets of the very wealthy, most of which are located abroad. This is a measure that is opposed by Western oligarchs, and not only by their reviled counterparts . . . Nevertheless, there is clear evidence that requisition, which may once have seemed a far-fetched or at least unrealistic concept, is in fact by no means impossible.

Somewhat earlier, in February 2022, an isolated and ostensibly anecdotal case made the headlines. Rotterdam city council announced their intention to dismantle a bridge built in 1927 (to say nothing of a previous one built half a century earlier), and classified as a national monument, in order to allow Jeff Bezos to sail his new superyacht, with its imposing three masts, out of the port. It seems that this absurd demand came close to being accepted, by a social-democrat mayor; moreover, in spite of the fact that in 2017, following renovation work, the bridge had been accorded protected status. The process was eventually halted thanks to a social protest movement, admittedly online, though threatening to take on a more physical manifestation in the form of a mass event in which rotten eggs would be hurled at the vessel. The incident was apparently finally resolved in July 2022, when the naval shipyard agreed to withdraw the request made to the town councillors. Nevertheless, the whole story speaks volumes about the extent of the power (a mix of symbolic recognition and the potential to influence) that our society unduly confers on material wealth.

Such one-off events, spectacular as they are, should not, however, distract attention from some deep-rooted and highly telling economic tendencies. The luxury yacht sector survived the global financial crisis, which began in 2007–2008, without any lasting ill effects, particularly at the top end of the market. The observation is even more striking in the context of the Covid-19 pandemic – or rather 'syndemic', to use the term proposed by Richard Horton, editor-in-chief of *The Lancet* and someone we shall encounter somewhat unexpectedly in the course of this book. Not only did the luxury yachting market emerge unscarred, but it was in fact almost boosted as a result of this challenge, as was the case with the wealth of billionaires in general. The sector was indeed flourishing in 2021, whether in the context of new sales or the second-hand market, sales and rentals, construction and refits. Order books were full (at the end of 2021, over 1,000 superyachts were on order, while almost 900 had been sold in the same year – almost twice as many as in 2020) and prices were on the rise. Over a more extended period, the growth of the sector since the 1980s reflects what Branko Milanović (2016) called 'the emergence of global plutocracy', with all that implies in terms of social separatism 'from the top'. Manufacturers were left in no doubt and willingly played up the card of a sound investment in the case of confinement – what better way to respect 'social distancing' in the best possible conditions. The superyacht would pass for the perfect incarnation of the concept of *liberté–délivrance* (freedom–release) analysed by the philosopher Aurélien Berlan (2021), if the frenzied quest for space by a few multibillionaires had not pushed the desire for an 'exit' even further . . .

Criticizing the lifestyle of the ultra-rich does not, however, always get a good press, including from those who denigrate socio-economic inequalities. For Louis Maurin (2021), director of the *Observatoire des inégalités* in France, focusing criticism on the ultra-rich means ignoring an affluent class who are less visible but more numerous. By limiting things to '1%', he argued, we are forgetting the 8% of 'wealthy people' (with individual earnings of more than 3,500 euros per month net after tax) and the 20% of 'privileged individuals' at the top level of social stratification in France. Unless the entire social structure is taken into account, criticizing the ultra-rich would be easy but not strictly pertinent. Such criticism of criticism, which also lambasts the myopia and even duplicity of an economically protected left-leaning intellectual bourgeoisie, deserves to be taken into account, even if only as a safeguard. It is true that a narrow focus on a handful of billionaires could result in a distorted view, both of class structure in general and of the mechanisms that generate inequalities. This approach nevertheless raises a number of problems, both from a sociological and from a political point of view. It places undue focus on inequalities in income rather than on inequalities in assets and *a fortiori* on inequalities within the relations of production. Furthermore, it ignores the considerable disparities existing within the very heart of the chosen categories and the dizzying extent to which wealth is monopolized by a very small number of individuals. Is it reasonable to criticize salary levels that, however high they may be in relative terms, are nevertheless justifiable in absolute terms and even represent a pay level to which all workers should be able to aspire without shame, while at the same time minimizing the gulf separating them from concentrations of wealth that are utterly indefensible?

With regard to the ecological aspect, Andreas Malm demonstrates that the distinction first suggested thirty years ago between 'luxury emissions' and 'subsistence emissions' (of CO_2), has lost nothing of its relevance and is, on the contrary, still pertinent today. Explicitly mentioning superyachts, he goes as far as to point out that luxury emissions are even less acceptable in the current situation and must therefore be regarded as a priority target. 'This is crime sold as ideal living' he declares (Malm, 2021, p. 91), referring to the encouragement of a consumption that, conspicuous though it may be, nevertheless remains destructive. Indeed, articles calling for an urgent focus on the damage caused by the lifestyles of the wealthiest individuals or social groups and their completely excessive carbon footprint can now be found in natural science publications as well as in those relating to the social sciences (Otto et al., 2019; Barros and Wilk, 2021; Chancel, 2022). Of course, putting a certain emphasis on superyachts in no way exonerates other forms of pollution, which are at least as damaging, such as, for example, those caused by cruise ships with their thousands of passengers. Clearly a whole range of practices, relating to both work and leisure, need to be re-examined. What is more, the problems caused by the lifestyle of the super-rich are definitely not confined to the sphere of consumption. In reality, they stem from both the social organization of production and from investment (in fossil fuels in particular), not to mention intense lobbying to steer the framing of the climate catastrophe to their own benefit (Morena, 2023).

A few words, finally, on the collection in which this book was published in French, since this explains the somewhat unusual style used in the book in comparison with traditional academic norms. Called *'L'ordinaire du capital'* (The everyday face of capital), this collection was initially intended to contribute to a critique of everyday life, as shaped by capitalism, through the publication of 'literary documents'. Since then, the collection has included literature, journalism and social science in a range of books which do not hesitate to mix genres or blur boundaries. This is the explanation behind the approach adopted in this book with its different written styles including first-person narrative, prosopopoeia and elements of mockery . . . It seemed to me, in fact, that the subject demanded an approach that was both serious and playful. It goes without saying, however, that humour in no way prevents a serious tone. A playground for the extravagantly luxurious boats belonging to a number of individuals, the Mediterranean is, at the same time, a place of death for others – the refugees and migrants who die at sea in their thousands each year while attempting to land their fragile vessels on the European coast.

The original subtitle was a somewhat provocative nod to the famous line *'Luxe, calme et volupté'* from Charles Baudelaire's poem 'L'invitation au voyage', and also an allusion to a painting of the same name by Henri Matisse, created in Saint-Tropez in 1904, when he was in the region as a guest of his fellow painter (and experienced yachtsman) Paul Signac. Which is also the place where the story begins . . .

Chapter 1

A colossus at anchor

I arrived via the main road that runs along the southern side of the bay, and parked in the carpark for the so-called new port. By the time I had stretched my legs after the journey I was already half-way between the fire station and the VIP Room, one of the fashionable discotheques in the area. I had two whole hours ahead of me for a carefully planned operation. Thoroughly caught up in what I had come to do, albeit still somewhat sceptical, I was about to take a close look at the boats moored along the quay, something I would never previously have dreamt of, given the extent to which anything relating to the open sea had always struck me as profoundly boring. Even more surprisingly, having already caught a distant glimpse of a huge vessel moored near the lighthouse, I was anticipating a really big prize. Until that moment, the sight of moored yachts, or rather, the sight of a tight knot of curious onlookers gaping at moored yachts, would have depressed me, yet here I was – one of them. Which goes to show that you should never pass up an opportunity to try out something new . . .

Indeed, it was not without a certain enthusiasm that I found myself heading towards the marina on this mild morning (the Côte d'Azur was certainly living up to the name first coined for it in 1887 by Stéphen Liégeard with both sky and sea of the promised colour). I even allowed myself time to stroll around a little, glancing at the signs advertising yacht hire, which I had walked past so many times before without even noticing. The offices were closed and the lights off but the advertisements remained clearly visible. With the idea that some visual image might be useful, I tried to take a photo but the glare made my reflection appear too clearly in the window display, as though it were superimposed. Evidently that was not going to work and, after a further and equally unsuccessful attempt, I gave up altogether, putting it off till later, though without any guarantee that I would come back the same way (and indeed, the opportunity never arose again).

For the moment, there were few people around. It was almost the last week in February and, at that time of year, the streets, though not deserted, are generally quiet. The peaceful atmosphere of the village was in sharp contrast to some of the stereotypes associated with the place. The image that comes to mind might perhaps be that of the artists, attracted to the area more than a century ago by the beauty of the light. In spite of changes that would have been inconceivable at that time, some traces of the colourful charm of the old days still linger. Standing in Rue de l'Annonciade, near the site of the eponymous museum, I could see down towards the port and its artists, this time looking perfectly in keeping with the cliché. On the opposite side of the road, like a distillation of historical change, a luxury boutique installed in an old Provençal villa dominated the square.

The area around the port was noticeably more animated, though still a far cry from its summer frenzy. Walking back along the quay, I briefly wondered about making a detour to visit the famous café, visually unmistakable thanks to its red facade. The purpose of my visit would not, however, be to pause for a drink but rather to update data collected in the context of ongoing research on social relationships in a peninsula regarded as a sociological vantage point. Part of this process involved checking prices *in situ* and, in particular, I was curious to know if the half-pint and pint of ordinary beer had respectively crossed the thresholds of ten and twenty euros. Nevertheless, I continued on my way, though not without a brief pause to take a look at *Sea Gull*, a regular sight here, forty metres long and built in 1980, as is evident from her vintage appearance, in spite of a recent three-year facelift.

In accordance with the narrative traditionally associated with this place, my thoughts should have turned first to Guy de Maupassant and to Paul Signac. Discovering the area for the first time in 1889 on board his yacht *Bel-Ami*, the former kept a daily record of his impressions in an account that was then immediately published. Paul Signac, himself a reader of Maupassant's book and a skilled yachtsman, succumbed to the charm of the place while on board *Olympia* a few years later, immortalizing it in a number of paintings such as *The Red Buoy* and *The Port at Sunset*. And yet, as I walked on, my thoughts turned instead to Emma Goldman who – a fact long forgotten by local history – wrote her memoirs here. When she concluded the acknowledgement section of *Living my Life* with the words 'Saint-Tropez, France, January 1931', she still had almost ten years of her life ahead of her and would die a long way from Saint-Tropez, in Toronto, in May 1940. Yet it was in Saint-Tropez, at the end of the 1920s, that she rediscovered her zest for life, and where, at the age of almost sixty, she even learned to swim. I could picture her, far from the Missouri cell where she had been confined a few years earlier, forced to write without any documentation since the prison authorities had confiscated thirty-five years of material. Like the writers and painters before her, she conjures up the charm of a picturesque fishing village. Even if a few traces of that still linger, the contrast between then and now cannot fail to provoke a smile. It is true that initially the region of Saint-Tropez was never really envisaged as a holiday destination, even for the winter months. Historians and geographers recall that at the end of the nineteenth century, this almost insular territory was generally regarded as remote and cut off, devoid of any potential for development.

In any case, I was not mistaken and the specimen visible at the end of the jetty was indeed a fine one. With its dazzling white surfaces, it would be hard to miss, even with so many other boats vying for attention. Although not yet capable of identifying such vessels at first glance, and indeed without any intention of becoming an expert in the field, I had no recollection of having previously seen this one, which, on a rough pacing out, appeared to be relatively long for a port that, in theory, has difficulty accommodating boats in excess of sixty meters. And I was right; *Neninka* was indeed a newcomer, as became clear from a subsequent check on a maritime geolocalization website. This new girl on the block (if we are to feminize boats in the English manner) was built in 2019; sixty-eight meters long, and sailing under the flag of the Cayman Islands (like the *Sea Gull* glimpsed a little earlier and many others besides), she had come from Monaco and would head back in the direction of Antibes. On the quay, in the shadow cast by the vessel, men in crew uniforms – those not fortunate enough to have a polo-shirt embossed with the name of the boat – were hard at work making everything gleam. One of them was busy cleaning a chrome strip with a toothbrush for the approval of unseen clients.

Chapter 2

One form of excess can conceal another

Let us speak frankly. After all, this is just between ourselves. What could seem more trivial than luxury yachting, alias superyachting? Surely only someone slightly weird, or even frankly irresponsible, could display any real interest in something so futile. Without nurturing a deep passion for sailing, underpinned by a somewhat perverted interest in the life of the super-rich, it would, *a priori*, be difficult to consider the subject as anything more than an insignificant phenomenon, of at best marginal interest, even if only in purely numerical terms. By definition, this is an activity that involves only an infinitesimal fraction of humanity, one whose lifestyle has almost literally been totally severed from any connection to the ordinary social world. At first sight, luxury yachting is so far removed from the ordinary that it concerns almost nobody.

In 2010, the editor of the influential scientific review *The Lancet*, Richard Horton (still in post ten years later), encouraged a relaxed approach to the question, at least in comparison with what was, in his view, the only subject that really matters – that of health. Unlike inequalities in terms of health, which are never a good thing, he argued that economic inequalities can prove to be beneficial, with the result that yachts should no longer be seen as a major evil and even – why not – should perhaps be regarded in a positive light. Move along folks, there's nothing to see here. Furthermore, ignorance tends to nourish the misconception according to which, once stripped of their most luxurious attributes, luxury yachts combine aesthetic taste and a concern for the environment – a noble activity in every sense of the term.

Whether in English or in French, media coverage, including in what are regarded as the quality papers, tends to adopt a benevolent, even indulgent, stance. (This was at least the case until the outbreak of the Covid-19 pandemic; admittedly, things have changed noticeably since then.) In general, accusations of immorality are rare, even though from a critical point of view, this is the weakest line of defence. In spite of their obvious efforts to maintain neutrality, or at least some semblance of it in their descriptions, not infrequently articles still portray the subject in an almost enchanted light. It is all too easy to imagine that these journalists would in truth very much like to be 'a part of it all' and certainly they appear undeterred by the sheer vulgarity it represents. Or else they are simply anxious not to cause any offence to the people involved so as to protect their own potential access, which amounts to the same thing. Such accounts vaunt the lure of wide-open spaces, the taste for fine materials, the appreciation of technological sophistication, the thrill of competitive sports, even perhaps a charming eccentricity . . . When any criticism is voiced, not only does it tend to be somewhat toned down, but it generally confines itself to ridiculing a specific whim, or to bemoaning a lack of restraint. The emphasis is placed on *excess* and nothing more. Luxury yachting? A magnifying glass focusing our gaze on an unrestrained taste for ostentation and delusions of grandeur; an exaggerated vagary of the super-rich with a tendency for extravagance. A trifle regrettable perhaps, but localized and inoffensive – time to move on.

Excess is, of course, all too easy to spot, and without even needing to venture into unsavoury territory, it is not difficult to find edifying stories of the kind where only an exceptional degree of *sang-froid* prevents the reader from mentally devising forms of retaliation not at all compatible with the moral principles they would normally apply.

One of the latest luxury yacht fads is for 'RainSky' shower units. They have shower heads the size of a car bonnet, consume 10 gallons of water a minute and cost €18,000. "Our clients finished with whirlpool baths a while back," said Matthias Voit whose company, Dornbach, makes the units, "they now want special showers in which you can control the droplet size and the speed at which they fall." Mr Voit said his latest order was from an unnamed Russian client who wanted a 'RainSky' shower on his yacht capable of squirting either water or champagne on demand. "We'll manage that," Mr Voit said. "The only unresolved question is whether the champagne should be warm or cold," he added. (*The Independent*, 3 February 2011)

And this is just one of many examples, even, as the date implies, in the midst of an economic 'crisis'. No need, in other words, to go to any special efforts to uncover extravagance and vanity: they reveal themselves quite openly. Even when some of those involved pride themselves on their cultural tastes, things can go awry:

A yachtsman with a keen interest in art may indeed derive a certain amount of pleasure in showing off his old masters to his guests. Yet it is a gesture that can turn out to be somewhat risky. At the start of the year, a Basquiat worth 110 million dollars and depicting a black skull on a blue background, was in urgent need of restoration after the children of the yacht owner, terrified by the painting, threw a bowl of cornflakes over

it. The crew's attempts to clean the canvas made the disaster
even worse. (*Le Monde*, 17 August 2019)

Whether this story provokes irritation or amusement (or a
mixture of the two), it nevertheless risks confining the subject
purely to the realm of the anecdotal. In a sense, it requires a
genuine effort to take superyachts seriously, if only for the
power of revelation conferred by dramatic facts or extraordinary phenomena.

One simple way of doing this is to take critical judgement
focusing on excess one step further, to the point where it coin-
cides with the idea of deviance. Viewed from this perspective,
superyachting can be regarded as a display of consumerism
and, through this, as an individual and social assertion that is
not only ostentatious but also pathological. All of which might
result in the whole subject being viewed as morally shock-
ing and socially obscene, an activity that should ultimately be
stopped, depending on the degree of repugnance such a pro-
hibition might provoke. This is undoubtedly an improvement
on simply feeling somewhat uneasy in the face of excessive
frivolity, but it does not go far enough. It is an argument
based on outgrowth and, as such, one which allows the source
responsible for it to be exonerated from any responsibility as
though it were simply a matter of proportion. Rather than
proceeding along this route, perhaps we should switch our
perspective altogether and challenge the accepted version of
things – somewhat in the way that Dubai, on a larger scale,
can be regarded as a stage of capitalism rather than as an
extravagant one-off. And, what if, instead of thinking in terms
of whims, of eccentricity, of excess, we use instead terms such
as reflection, expression, symptom? We would then be referring to a touchstone, rather than an anomaly, to a reliable
sample and not to an aberration. Superyachts? A measurement
device of sorts – a way of taking stock of the general frenzy
known as the 'normal' social order.

Once you adopt it, this standpoint proves fairly intuitive, doesn't it? For we clearly sense that the superyacht industry, with a financial weight currently estimated in excess of 25 billion dollars, reveals something about the capitalist system, at the very least by way of a startling summary. As early as 1993, Georges Hughes, a Scottish geographer, was perceptive enough to identify what the boom in superyachting might reveal. He saw it as a 'cultural symptom of the globalization of capitalism', yet, without losing sight of the inevitable materiality of that very symptom, simultaneously product and producer of a geographical reconfiguration compressing both time and space. When, more than fifteen years later, David Harvey used yachts to illustrate the relationship of cause and effect between the crackdown on wages affecting the majority and the purchase of luxury goods by the happy few ('go to any marina in Florida or around the Mediterranean, look at the yachts and cruise boats moored there, then contrast this with what you would have seen in 1970 and you will get the point'), this was simply a passing remark in the context of a commentary on the role of effective demand in the circulation of capital. The author was, moreover, focusing attention on investment rather than on consumption, however ostentatious. Nevertheless, the example was not selected randomly. As a concrete illustration of the class struggle, it would be difficult to find anything better. Equally, it is all too clear that luxury yachting contributes to the creation of what Mike Davis and Daniel Monk described as 'evil paradises', which seem to epitomize the complete antithesis of a 'global slum', but always in the 'worst of worlds', in which a few dozen or a few hundred people own as much as almost four billion human beings.

It is not because luxury vessels remain outside the reach of ordinary people that they exist somehow outside the world. Similarly, socio-spatial separatism does not mean that the lifestyles of the wealthiest do not reshape the surrounding territories and landscapes. Here, as elsewhere, the dignity of the newly popular slogan depends on simply turning things round so that, rather than the world of superyachts, it is a case of superyachts *and their world*. Is luxury yachting simply an absurdity? Looked at more closely, it represents a condensed form of some of the essential traits that characterize our era: the steep rise in economic inequalities, the acceleration of ecological disaster and ongoing injustice within the legal system. It reinforces our awareness of the intensification of spatial segregation and fuels the debate around the constitution of a transnational dominant class. It brings us, in fact, to the very heart of such arguments, to the central core, where all of them intertwine.

A handful of super-rich individuals amuse themselves at sea ... So what? So . . . everything.

Chapter 3

Floating palaces

Size matters. According to the specialized literature, it constitutes the principal, and perhaps only, criterion. To be classed
as a superyacht, a threshold must be crossed. For a long time,
this was fixed at 24 meters and, in France, anything above
this qualifies as a superyacht. 'Super' perhaps, but statistically
insignificant, since for the last fifteen years at least this sector
has accounted for approximately 0.0085% of all boats registered in France – tax evasion undoubtedly playing its part. On
a worldwide scale, that 24 meters increasingly extends to 30,
a shifting yet critical marker distinguishing a superyacht from
a mere yacht. Clearly, an ongoing drive for increased length
means the established norms are constantly changing. Beyond
that figure are the mega-yachts (50, 60 or 75 meters) and the
giga-yachts (80, 90 or 100 meters). Definitions that scarcely
follow any fixed norms and that are, so to speak, extremely
fluid.

Maximum and average lengths are indeed constantly
increasing, even if around three quarters of the worldwide
fleet of superyachts remain below the 45-meter threshold. In
1990, a boat of this length was enough to place you in the top
one hundred. Scarcely a quarter of a century later the figure

was at least 75 meters, whereas 45 meters was simply the average length of the total fleet. And the average length of the one hundred largest vessels is now close to a hundred meters, in other words, the length of a rugby or soccer pitch. Boats are getting ever longer and ever bigger – and, it goes without saying, ever more expensive. Healthy competition, according to the professionals representing the high end of the sector, who regard this competitive element as highly entertaining, or in other words highly profitable.

At the last count, in the spring of 2020, the prize went to *Azzam* with her 180 meters. The interior of the boat, owned by the President of the United Arab Emirates, is reputed to be fitted out in a more relaxed version of Empire style. In any case, *Azzam* succeeded in supplanting *Eclipse* with its 162.5 meters (with *Dubai* hard on its heels, at less than a meter difference – here, as elsewhere, competition sometimes comes down to a hair's breadth), owned by the Russian billionaire Roman Abramovich, one of the best-known enthusiasts in the field and a collector (he owns, or has owned, *Pelorus*, *Grand Bleu* or *Ectasea*, respectively 115, 113 and 86 meters). *Fulk Al Salaman*, acquired by the royal family of the Sultanate of Oman, slipped into second place and, at 155 meters, *Al Saïd* was not far behind . . . And this hierarchy, always on the point of being shaken up and rapidly becoming obsolete, must be treated with caution. (The same is true moreover, when it comes to naming the first superyacht in history: there is no consensus on the subject. *Christiana O*, a yacht belonging to Aristotle Onassis is often cited, but *The New York Times* first used the term as early as 1928 to describe Vincent Astor's *Nourmahal* as a craft heralding 'a new era'.) While *Dilbar*, a newcomer to the race, may not be the longest yacht in the world, its thousands of square meters of habitable space (for less than twenty passengers) mean that it can, on the other hand, claim to be the largest in terms of internal volume . . . a claim disputed, however, by *Double Century*. In any event, alongside these, Steven Spielberg's *Seven*

Seas (86 meters); *Dragonfly* (73 meters), owned by Sergey Brin, cofounder of Google; and, even more, *Vajoliroja* (48 meters), bought by Johnny Depp in 2006 and 're-vamped' in an art deco style (it would later be acquired and subsequently re-sold by the writer J.K. Rowling under its original name *Amphitrite*); are almost dwarfed. All things being equal, the same could be said of *Octopus* owned by the late Paul Allen, co-owner of Microsoft, despite the fact that, with its 126 meters, it took pole position in 2003 in the category of superyachts designed to explore the far corners of the globe. It still continues to attract attention and is, without doubt, the most extraordinary superyacht in the world, at least according to recent comments by a military enthusiast, who would very much have liked to have had the means to buy it himself – although it would have cost him at least 325 million dollars. In terms of length, on the other hand, it is a third less than *Azzam* . . . all of which gives an indication of the current trend.

Incidentally, even *Azzam* may well start to feel somewhat less impressive. The 200-meter mark is proving to be too much of a temptation and there has been talk of it being overtaken on several occasions. And comfortably overtaken too, given that the new giant, recently announced, promises to be in the order of 220 meters. Back in 2015, there was talk of the construction of *Triple Deuce*, 222 meters long and costing a billion dollars, although this has apparently so far not progressed beyond the project stage. In 2017, it was the turn of a project entitled, provisionally at least, *Quintessentially One*, backed by a handful of billionaires keen to preserve their anonymity. A vessel so enormous, it was rumoured, that it would be unable to make a stopover in the port of Monte Carlo. A perfect spot to celebrate the birthdays of stars who have cultivated the right friendships, it would also serve as a hotel during events such as the Monaco Grand Prix, which, along with the Cannes film festival, marks the start, in May, of the summer season in the fashionable international calendar.

If increased length is a sign of distinction, it is a distinction based on imitation. Even if it means losing sight of the original purpose or intention of such concepts, what we are seeing here is more in the nature of a mimetic rivalry or an unmistakable mimicry, in the guise of the most ostentatious form of competition; a competition where the most basic practical rationality is sometimes ignored, since the biggest vessels are quite simply too big to enter some of the most popular ports.

Yet size is by no means everything. To complete the picture, two additional criteria must be met, in addition to that of private ownership, which without exactly being a *sine qua non*, almost always applies, in that the few superyachts that are ostensibly reserved for political functions or positions are, in reality, privatized.

Criterion number one: the presence on board of a professional crew. As a general rule, these slightly outnumber the passengers, a ratio that tends to increase as the boats get proportionally longer. Typically, on a boat of fifty to sixty meters in length, there will be ten, twelve or fifteen passengers with about twenty crew members at their service. Almost without exception, the captains are men (as is also the case incidentally for the owners of the fifty largest vessels), in contrast with the female hairdressers, masseuses, nannies or chefs who keep things running smoothly behind the scenes.

Criterion number two: the capacity to move freely across international zones. We should pause for a moment – so to speak – to examine this notion of mobility. A far cry from the castle of former times, synonymous with immobility and with a domination firmly rooted in a local territory, this ability to disregard common frontiers while at the same time preserving a distance from ordinary people, is currently a typical element of the lifestyle of the dominant classes and, in particular, of the wealthiest among them. The presence of a heliport (sometimes even two, as on the already mentioned *Octopus*) represents an unmistakable sign of the hypermobility characteristic of a 'global super-bourgeoisie'. Superyacht, helicopter: each corresponds, whether at sea or in the air, to different speed regimes, each with its own specific purposes, but both have in common the flouting of borders by creating an exclusive space, with the guarantee of perfect privacy. This space is not strictly speaking deterritorialized but rather characterized by a multi-faceted and global territorialization. And, it might be added, a superficial one. Using resources drawn from ethnography, geographer Emma Spence argues that the assertion of status takes precedence over locomotion in so far as the show of hypermobility is, in practical terms, extremely limited, and even illusory, because in reality confined to a small number of privileged spaces: a spatial concentration which, furthermore, only exacerbates mimetic rivalry.

This hypermobility is therefore as much expressive as it is instrumental. Superyachts represent both a means and a sign. The expressive dimension has, moreover, been a feature of the luxury yachting world from its modern origins in the middle of the nineteenth century, among the upper classes, putting it more or less in line with other elite sports and hobbies. Being a member of a 'yacht club' therefore allows certain individuals, generally members of an upwardly mobile business middle class, to indicate their affiliation to the 'elite'. We can see this as the new manifestation of an old phenomenon: what Max Weber described, when referring to luxury in the context of the feudal ruling class as 'the means of its social self-assertion'. The fact remains that, in concrete terms, the relationship between mobility and immobility has become a major component of relations of domination within the working of neoliberal capitalism. The 'new spirit of capitalism' of the late twentieth century explored by Luc Boltanski and Ève Chiapello more than twenty years ago was distinguished by, among other things, 'the generalization of a balance of forces bound up with mobility': 'Great men do not stand still. Little people remain rooted to the spot. Those with power do not remain in one place. Those without it stay where they are.' Today that 'spirit', as it was described then, is, to some extent, obsolete. It has reinvented itself but, on this precise point, the argument still holds. We can go even further back in time to find other examples of this power to flout ordinary frontiers. In 1967, Henri Lefebvre observed, 'Who can ignore that the Olympians of the new bourgeois aristocracy no longer inhabit. They go from grand hotel to grand hotel, or from castle to castle, command a fleet or a country from a yacht. They are everywhere and nowhere.'

Sheer size, presence of staff, mobility – this trilogy represents the defining features associated with superyachts and distinguishes them both from cruise ships and ordinary pleasure craft. As is made very clear in a repeatedly used and even hackneyed description, reproduced in dozens, if not hundreds, of newspaper articles over the course of the last forty years, and referring to the British royal family's yacht *Britannia*, or to *Nabila* (formerly owned by the late Saudi Arabian arms dealer Adnan Khashoggi and later renamed as *Trump Princess* under the attentive care of another wheeler-dealer), superyachts are 'floating palaces', not floating 'cities'. Cruise ships may indeed measure more than 300 meters and house swimming pools, restaurants, bars, cinemas or theatres; they nevertheless host several thousand people. Quite the opposite of a superyacht, where only the very largest have the capacity to carry more than twenty passengers.

The privilege of the select few is a defining feature of luxury yachting. The challenge of the pandemic has, if need be, clarified matters, and the ocean liners transformed into viral 'clusters' are worlds apart from the peaceful seclusion afforded by the superyacht. And this also distinguishes superyachting from ordinary yachting, an activity which, over the last few decades, has seen a massive expansion, or a 'democratization' as it has sometimes rather misguidedly been termed, thereby further stripping the term of any of its subversive power and even of any genuine meaning. Research on yachting generally highlights the spread down the social ladder of a practice that was in the past, at least until the postwar years, the preserve of a wealthy elite. Such research charts a significant expansion from the 1960s onwards, resulting in a level that, in France today, includes several million occasional or regular practitioners of sailing or water-based sports. And, in this context, attention is also focused on the significant number of white-collar and blue-collar workers, who, in 2016, represented 14.5% of all new registrations in terms of ownership. A very far cry from the microcosm with which we are concerned here.

Chapter 4

Specimens

> *Bad Girl* (formerly *Chamar*). 1992 (refitted: 2013). 56.7 m.
> 18–25 knots.
> 6 cabins. 12 passengers, 14 crew members.
> Summer rates: $225,000 per week.
> Winter rates: $205,000 per week.
> Flag: Bermuda

I may indeed be a bad girl (I prefer the word naughty but I leave you to be the judge of that), but, with my modest length of barely 57 meters, nobody can accuse me of harbouring delusions of grandeur. I don't even get a mention on the Wikipedia page of the world's largest yachts, which incidentally I would recommend you approach with a pinch of salt. I am three times smaller than those monsters on the podium . . . and slender into the bargain. Restrained. Like my rates: in the summer I can be hired for 225,000 dollars per week and, in low season, for a mere 205,000 . . . peanuts! After all, if you want to cruise around some little corner of paradise at a speed of at least 15 knots, you have to put in a little effort. You'd be handing over a million to hire *Eclipse* or *Barbara*, so in comparison . . . Burgess, the same broker that looks after me, and one of the largest in the market, offers *Capri*, scarcely any longer than me, for around 340,000 dollars per week. When all is said and done, I'm a bargain. For, as well as being modest, I am well equipped. Sports room (yoga-friendly, it goes without saying), steam room, jacuzzi – the full works – not to mention my giant plasma screen. If the passengers, a maximum of twelve, fail to agree on the film, each of them can enjoy their own little personal cinema or play video games in their cabins. Needless to say, I am fully equipped with everything anyone could want, from tenders to jet-skis; even fishing equipment for those who still like that kind of thing. My extra-wide upper deck, which serves as a solarium, is certainly a factor when it comes to my popularity. Built in 1992 – at the time, I was called *Chamar* – I am by no means past it, particularly as I was rebuilt in 1995 and then completely refitted less than ten years later. Always where the action is, I am a regular visitor to the French Riviera.

All right, of course I cannot compete with the most outlandish vessels. Some of them have – in no particular order – a concert hall big enough to hold an entire orchestra, a hospital wing and medical centre (complete with operating theatre), a mosque, a wine cellar full of top vintages, an extra-large sports centre, an auditorium, a recording studio, an outdoor cinema, a tennis court and even a small golf course, an anti-paparazzi security system, a missile defence system (you simply cannot be too careful) or a James Bond style mini submarine, where appropriate shaped like a shark (one of the enthusiasts in this field even has a reputation for naming his boats with reference to 007 and then quickly selling them on once he has bought them), sprung-floored corridors – any combination of the above is possible. Let's just say that I favour a somewhat more modest approach, relatively speaking. Anyway, what the majority of clients want more than anything else is a giant TV.

Many of my fellow vessels prefer the Cayman Islands but, having been built by a British company, my fiscal paradise and flag of convenience is Bermuda.

*

> *Solandge.* 2013 (refit 2019). 85 m. 15 knots.
> 7–8 cabins. 12–16 passengers. 28 crew members.
> Summer rates: 1m. euros per week.
> Winter rates: 1 m. dollars per week.
> Flag: Malta.

The interior of *Solandge* would delight Tutankhamun, Catherine the Great, Liberace and Tony Soprano combined, joked a *Daily Telegraph* journalist. Hilarious. I love it when hacks display a sense of humour.

Well, it's true that on the interior decoration front, things could have been a little more restrained. From the outside, it might not be obvious, given that my streamlined hull, the work of a Norwegian designer, was awarded the prize for the most beautiful exterior at the 2014 Monaco Yacht Show – the ultimate accolade. In contrast, it must be admitted, the interior is, well, somewhat ornate. Words can scarcely do it justice. An illuminated 15-meter sculpture representing the tree of life, a pronounced penchant for amethyst . . . The dining room television screen may indeed be concealed behind a painting and the windows of the owners' suite decorated with murals on the theme of the garden of Eden – innocence, my guilty pleasure – but none of that is quite enough to make people take me more seriously. Never mind the kitsch, however, the most important thing is a sense of wellbeing. And from that perspective, you've come to the right place. My showpiece is the top deck, with its wooden floor and central jacuzzi. Since this is where the parties happen, the jacuzzi converts into a dance floor. That means that, when required, the number of people can go up from twelve to sixty. Spread over five more stepped decks, there is a swimming pool, a sauna, a hammam, a hydrotherapy centre, a cinema, a wine cellar ... you name it. My stabilization system, designed to reduce roll, ensures a maximum level of comfort. And, on top of all that, plenty of flunkeys, sorry – staff, or rather colleagues, ready to be of service

We make it happen – the simple pleasure of seeing one's family having a good time, the peaceful joy of gathering friends together, this is what I offer. Our motto: 'When you have achieved everything in life, only generosity remains.' Brilliant, isn't it? Of course, philanthropy does not come cheap: a million dollars a week, and that is in the cold season when I am in the Caribbean. In the summer, when I sail around Monaco and Sardinia, it is still a million, but euros this time. Not including fuel: twenty litres per kilometre, roughly speaking. Whatever it takes ...

*

> *A (Motor Yacht A)*. 2008. 118–119 m. 19–23 knots.
> 7 cabins. 14 passengers. 42 crew members.
> Approximate value: around 325 million $.
> Flag: Marshall Islands/Bermuda.

A, that's my name. Nothing to do with anarchy, as you might guess. No need to panic: A is the initial of the first name of the wife of my owner, a Russian banker by the name of Andrey Melnichenko, a recent arrival on the list of the one hundred richest people in the world according to *Forbes*. On a more serious note, the name means the vessel is always at the beginning of any alphabetical list and therefore first on the registers. You do whatever it takes to make sure you get noticed. That said, when it comes to asserting myself, it's hardly my style to play coy. And even less so now, since I have recently acquired a double identity.

First of all, as a motor yacht. A little less than 120 meters (sometimes cited as up to 150 meters, since people are simply incapable of showing any restraint). Although not necessarily on the subject of length, I have to admit that I have not escaped controversy. I've been accused of looking like a submarine, but we'll let that pass. What I have found less easy to accept is that people jeer at my bar made of Baccarat crystal and my swimming pool – one of my swimming pools – which has a glass bottom, enabling swimmers to be seen from the below-deck discotheque – that is when it is not being used as a garage for speed boats. For something worth in excess of 300 million dollars and around forty crew members (and as many video-surveillance cameras – security is key), a certain amount of equipment is required. But, if I am something of a star, it is above all because I was designed by Philippe Starck himself. To tell the truth, I can't say that means very much to me, but clearly it is a name that impresses people. And, after all, it was he who designed Port Adriano in Majorca, known for its super-chic and ultramodern atmosphere. When I, who am perfectly capable of breaking icebergs on my travels, turn up in some unlikely place like Dinard or Saint-Malo, as I did in September 2016, I can assure you that my visit does not go unremarked. Yes, all right, I consume around 2,000 litres of fuel per hour and it takes almost a million and a half dollars to fill the tank. But you should see the sheer class of it all! I don't sail, I glide, imperceptibly and without the hint of a splash. So smoothly in fact, that Steve Jobs, cofounder of Apple, hired this Starck fellow to design his own plaything, or the interior at least. That was *Venus*, 79 meters long, 100 million euros, including nine million for the designer, who kicked up quite a stink because he ended up only getting six. As for Jobs, he was unlucky; the poor man (in a manner of speaking) died before he could take advantage of his boat, sleekly designed along the lines of an *Apple Store*.

As for me, I am in such good shape that I have now taken up sailing. After *Motor Yacht A*, make way for *Sailing Yacht A*. Same letter, same stylist, same owner – why change a winning team? My fame is unlikely to diminish since, with my 143 meters, I am reputed to be the biggest private sailing yacht on this entire planet. With enough space for twenty passengers and a staff of about fifty minions. Which is why the bill is a little steep, with a purchase price of over 400 million euros. But when you look at what you get: eight decks, a helipad and a submarine, an underwater observation room . . . and the *must*: the glass railing on the main deck, 1.8 tons, according to some, the largest single piece of glass ever made. And, in addition, I could almost qualify as eco(logical), with my hybrid propulsion system – what a joke! When I turn up, people have eyes only for me with my carbon masts soaring more than one hundred meters above the waterline. Eat your heart out Big Ben and your chimes!

Chapter 5

UHNWI

It could easily be mistaken for the English acronym for a branch of the United Nations but, in fact, it is nothing of the sort. UHNWI stands for ultra-high-net-worth individuals. Leaving any poetry aside, UHNWIs are the top echelon of otherwise common or garden HNWIs. An 'ultra' disappears and a yawning chasm opens up. As Anglo-American as it may seem, the acronym has some French blood in its veins: it was first coined by the French multinational Capgemini, in association with the American investment bank, Merrill Lynch.

In the jargon of those in high places, the type of people featured, for example, in *Forbes* magazine, which, in 1982, launched a list of the wealthiest people in the world, subsequently widely imitated, this acronym refers to individuals whose personal net worth is in excess of thirty million US dollars. An arbitrary classification, of course, and one that has provoked criticism and rivalries (as the stakes get higher, the threshold is sometimes fixed at 50 million), but that has nevertheless established itself. Expressions like super-rich and ultra-rich are no longer confined to activist declamations or essays and opinion pieces. Even in serious academic publications on the subject, numbers of which have increased over the last fifteen years, such terms have begun to appear, as though conceptual sophistication was in danger of muddying the waters. Provoking strong reactions, the category of 1% is also deceptive, sociologically speaking, given that it effectively shows even more disparity than the remaining 99%. Trying to situate our UHNWIs within such a broad sample, compels them to rub shoulders with the destitute, relatively speaking. The rule of the decimal requires several zeros after the decimal point. Exactly 0.003% of the population, according to calculations made by the specialized company Wealth-X, who, in a report dated 2016, estimated the figure at around 212,000 people. Three years later, according to the same source, that figure had crossed a new threshold of more than 265,000 people. And the number continued to show a marked increase, by around 60% between 2005 and 2015, a period ostensibly shaken by a financial 'crisis'. The estimate for 2023 put the figure at 350,000. More generously, at the end of 2019, the British agency Knight Frank had already calculated the figure as more than 500,000. If we raise the entry threshold from fifty to one hundred million dollars, the pool becomes more restricted, of course, but the upward tendency is more pronounced. Fewer and fewer people, more and more money.

This represents a potentially promising market, given that the vast majority have yet to experience the pleasure of super-yachting, or have done so only in a sporadic and indirect way, by chartering (or simply by invitation) rather than as owners. This is particularly true in those countries described in the language of world capitalism as 'emerging'. The professionals within the sector are torn. On the one hand, the potential for growth is mouth-watering, since more than 90% of the super-rich are still to be conquered. But, on the other hand, this represents a considerable challenge and the dynamic of the market still relies on a small number who have 'heavily' invested. A 'Superyacht Industry Manifesto', published at the beginning of 2020, describes this delicate balance:

Quite simply, without an engaged group of ultra-high-net-worth individuals (UHNWIs) the superyacht industry would cease to exist, and for a number of years now the market has, for the most part, been kept afloat by repeat buyers from the same nations.

Russian oligarchs, leading figures from the leisure or entertainment industry, Silicon Valley tycoons, the kings of the oil, property or pharmaceutical sector – these effectively represent the restricted recruitment pool of superyachting. Only the very wealthiest can boast the price of admission and this epitomizes 'the pinnacle of experiential luxury' as it is described in the benchmark report, *The State of Wealth, Luxury and Yachting* (using the language of empiricist philosophy the better to transform material consumption into a sensory experience).

Clearly, this activity is not – and this is a huge understatement – within everyone's means. A frequently cited figure, apparently based on calculations made by the Wealth-X group and by the yachting company Camper & Nicholsons International, put the average value of a superyacht at around ten million dollars in 2010. A third, therefore, of the threshold that marks entry to UHNWI territory. In certain cases, estimating the cost of a vessel ends up being down to guesswork or even rumours. Even for the largest or most well-known vessels, valuations vary and figures need to be treated with caution. Valued at a price of 350 million dollars on construction, *Eclipse* subsequently weighed in at 500, 650, sometimes even 800 million dollars. In the case of *Azzam*, the initial price was estimated at 400 million dollars, then at 600, and finally according to a subsequent approximate assessment, at around 850 million dollars. *Rising Sun*, acquired by the producer David Geffen, and worth close to 600 million dollars today, was previously estimated at only around half that price. The taste for confidentiality is such that several of the longest boats, like *Flying Fox* (137 meters), were dreamt up and put together in secret, and under code names, before they were officially launched. In other cases, it was the names of the owners that were kept secret.

Discretion also competes with ostentation when it comes to displaying prices. For yachts of over forty meters, and particularly above that length, prices readily disappear from catalogues. These are matters to be discussed between civilized people. Making inquiries on the subject and asking about the price not only demonstrates poor taste but also sends a negative signal, implying that the necessary funds may be lacking (the saying according to which asking the price means revealing that you do not have the means, is attributed to former 'robber baron' John P. Morgan). Incidentally it is not necessarily easy, for the untrained eye, to distinguish between the genuine super-rich and those who are simply wealthy. Geographer Emma Spence, previously mentioned here, had an unpleasant experience of this type when she was researching for her PhD. Having worked for six years as a ground-based crew member in a brokerage agency in Florida, she considered herself well placed to identify potential clients during demonstrations. The experience revealed that, in reality, she was not quite as well equipped as she had thought. As well as familiarity with the technical vocabulary or knowledge of the various routes, you must also be able to judge appearances while at the same time accept being judged in return. That implies a level of cultural capital that is not only sufficient but appropriate and the ability to handle certain codes deftly. In her own case, as she describes, her lack of knowledge of luxury products led her to make a number of mistakes. More inclined to be relaxed than formal, the appearance of the wealthiest individuals does not necessarily correspond to stereotypes.

If being a mere multimillionaire is not enough, it is because the cost of buying the vessel is by no means the only aspect to be taken into account. Far from it. There is also maintenance and upkeep to consider. The annual cost of a superyacht is generally calculated as being roughly equivalent to 10% of the purchase price. A sum of several million dollars per year, therefore, just to be able to use it. When it comes to fuel, costs vary, but, as an order of magnitude, you would be looking at a figure of 500 litres for each hour of sailing for a boat of around seventy meters, in other words, around 400,000 dollars per year. Add to that mooring fees and insurance, not to mention the cost of internal fitting and decor. All of that amounts to a total of several thousand dollars per square meter for something relatively modest, and up to tens of thousands for anything else. The 'combined annual spending on the world's 6,281 superyachts could wipe out all developing countries' debts', journalist Rupert Neate noted in passing, in a 2018 article. Some years later, this observation still stands.

It is hardly surprising then that, in his portrait of 'the rich' spanning a period of several centuries, English journalist John Kampfner specifically takes us from ownership of slaves to ownership of superyachts. The fact is that the dramatic boom in the superyacht industry from the 1980s onwards is one of the most striking indications of the sharp rise in very high incomes and asset values throughout the world since that period, and of the resulting dramatic increase in deprivation. If there is indeed a single observation to be made concerning the widening in inequalities over the course of the last decades, it is that this has been exacerbated from above, fuelled less by increased salary levels – admittedly indefensibly high – than by the growth in asset values.

Of course, philanthropy is to be commended, or more recently, the current enthusiasm for the so-called 'sharing economy', as exemplified by an American company that broke new ground in this domain with a project called 'Instant Yachtification'. This is based on a system of shared ownership in exchange for being able to take advantage of the vessel for at least three weeks per year. But, ask the Saint-Tropez branch of the *Société nationale de sauvetage en mer* (equivalent to the British RNLI or US Coast Guard), struggling to carry out its mission due to lack of funds, if the yacht owners make even the smallest contribution, and the answer will be that, over the course of fifteen years, they have received nothing whatsoever. Various appeals for funds were made, without success, until, in October 2019, a former L'Oréal boss made some amends by signing a substantial cheque.

Chapter 6

Yachting lifestyle

Superyachting is a social world. A miniature one admittedly, but a social world nonetheless. It has its handbooks and its magazines, its symposiums and its shows, its clubs and its celebrities, its consultants and its captains. It even has its academic specialisms, such as one dedicated to design at Southampton Solent University, in the south of England, and, less surprisingly, one at the International University of Monaco, a business school, which offers five different specialisms – finance, luxury, marketing, sport and management – a splendid programme indeed. In order to be a member of this social world, a certain number of obligations must be met (in 2016, *The Financial Times* offered a user guide for potential buyers), but once these minor obstacles have been overcome, enthusiasts will tell you that luxury yachting is not just an experience, still less a simple activity. Much more than these, it is a complete lifestyle.

This (sales) argument – a word which tends to be wrongly substituted for that of argumentation, of which it is merely the commercial adulteration – is for example the creed preached by *Forbes*, well versed in the subject since the Forbes family own their own superyacht, *Highlander*, also enjoyed by Mick

Jagger and by Ronald Reagan. In 2019, an article in the magazine spelled it out plainly: superyachting = lifestyle. True, the author was simply reiterating the words of the boss of Camper & Nicholsons, one of the heavyweights within the sector and with every possible interest in establishing this perspective. And it is indeed already firmly established, not to say hackneyed. Thirty years ago, 'The Yachting Lifestyle' was used as an advertising slogan for *Yachting Magazine* – also in collaboration with *Forbes*.

All you need to explore the French Riviera is a yacht and a competent crew, as a practitioner explained in 2006, with undisguised enthusiasm. Having taken up residence in Nice, he described the joy of sailing, in the course of a single day, from a lively café in Saint-Tropez to a peaceful retreat off the island of Porquerolles, via the beach clubs of Pampelonne. And, if it should ever cross your mind that all this is a little trivial or unreal, there is always, he adds, some kind soul ready to reassure you: the purr of the engines, rather like the leather seats in a Ferrari, is certainly tangible enough. And therefore real. Sometimes, however, showiness is not appropriate. That huge black car forming a dark blot against the light once savoured by the impressionist painters usually belongs to a broker, whereas the yacht's owner or renter can perfectly choose to wander about the quay, incognito, dressed in shorts, an ice-cream in his hand. That is the magic of chartering. For the space of a week, you can be treated like a king.

So, what do you have to do? Nothing could be easier. Simply rent *Harmony*. Only 35 meters long but in perfect taste. The captain will welcome you aboard with a glass of champagne, while one of the hostesses takes care of your luggage and that of your friends. Monaco here we come. On the way, you could stop at the Ephrussi-de-Rothschild villa and gardens at Saint-Jean-Cap-Ferrat, home to the *Les Azuriales* opera festival, before enjoying a gastronomic dinner in the open air. The following day, a limousine could drive you to Château Eza, a five-star hotel. The next day, Saint-Tropez, with no traffic jams or motorway tolls and, who knows, you might find yourself being photographed by paparazzi on the beach at Pampelonne. In the evening, the Saint-Tropez nightclubs await – expect to spend something in the order of a few thousand, even tens of thousands, of euros. And no problem if you are overcome with fatigue and prefer to dine 'simply' on board, with a little something concocted for you by the chef.

Certainly, the *Telegraph* journalist, jauntily wearing his other hat as a consultant specializing in luxury would hardly have had the bad taste to dispute this advice. He describes with spellbound delight 'the secret world of the elite' on board the *Axioma*, 72 meters long, 635,000 euros a week in high winter season, not including food, drinks, fuel and all the rest. He waxes lyrical about the tropical fruits, the fresh pistachio muffins served for breakfast and pre-dinner cocktails on remote islands. Not only does he find nothing at all worth criticizing (except to note that they sometimes encountered other large boats – honestly, what a nerve!), but it is clear that he dreams of stepping into his hosts' shoes.

So, what is the main advantage of this mode of transport? Contrary to what the lay person might think, it is much less restrictive than a private jet. Of course, the latter has the advantage of speed which is ideal from a work point of view. But the downside is the very strict security rules. Almost suffocating in fact, for those seeking freedom of movement. You can of course work in a private jet, but in a superyacht, you can work *and* relax. Many of those at the top will confirm this, even if it sometimes turned out to be at their peril. In 2008, David Cameron found himself in hot water because the press tycoon Rupert Murdoch had invited him onto his superyacht, *Rosehearty*, via his private plane, so they could hold relaxed talks in a secluded spot on the Aegean. As it happened, the story did not seem to do much lasting harm to the leader of the Conservative Party, who became Prime Minister two years later. In 2017, it was former president Barack Obama who caused ripples among social media circles when he was photographed, while himself taking pictures of his wife Michelle, on board the yacht owned by the producer David Geffen, alongside other guests including the actor Tom Hanks, the singer Bruce Springsteen and the TV talk show host, Oprah Winfrey. In France, the prize goes, of course, to the former President, Nicolas Sarkozy, who did much to popularize the anglicism *bling-bling*, when on the evening of his election, while celebrating at Fouquet's, he accepted an offer made by Vincent Bolloré, one of the wealthiest individuals in France, inviting him to take a well-deserved break at the start of his presidency, as a guest on his private yacht, travelling there on his host's private plane.

Believe it or not, the staff are not always quite so captivated. Their voices go largely unheard and they are reluctant to speak for fear of reprisals, but the little information that filters through reveals the other side of the dream. A heavily disciplined side, made up of punishing working hours and an enforced docility, squeezed into tiny cabins and often obliged to work intense shifts in order to provide a round-the-clock service. And all that with a permanent smile on their faces, even in the face of the most preposterous whims. 'Yachting lifestyle' for some; 'golden exploitation' for others. In the waters of the Caribbean, a woman demanded the immediate delivery of a thousand white roses to decorate the superyacht belonging to her husband. The staff had them flown in by helicopter from Miami. She then wanted to get rid of them just as quickly the following day. Reluctant to throw them into the ocean, they had to keep them in their cramped quarters. In general, reports hint at pressure of all kinds, from the repetition of exhausting tasks to sexual harassment, bringing with it an inevitable toll of depression and even suicide.

Sceptics have therefore claimed that slaving away on a superyacht can be just as dangerous as working on an oil rig. Injuries and accidents are by no means rare and, if they appear to be unusual, it is only because they are covered up or are classed as accidents rather than the result of any negligence, a process that eliminates any possibility of legal action.

And, like tax fraud, such incidents are unlikely to attract much enthusiasm from the police. When a problem does arise, it is often met with a complex legal maze, involving international waters, untraceable owners, and flags of convenience. In terms of labour law, superyachts are a law unto themselves, completely outside any territorial jurisdiction. Yet such accidents can sometimes be fatal. In 2010, Will Black, a crew member and bosun on board a superyacht, disappeared in Monaco, apparently as the result of a collision. It is difficult to know exactly what happened because, without any attempt to look into the incident, the captain simply reported his disappearance and handed over his personal possessions to the police before promptly weighing anchor. His body was never found. In 2013, a young man named Michael Hanlon drowned in Antibes, after falling from his ship unnoticed while trying to get back on board at night. His body was found the day after he disappeared. In another incident in 2017, crew member Jacob Nichol died after two years in a critical condition following a serious fall sustained while cleaning the superyacht, on which he was supposedly working as an assistant engineer, for the very first time. There are almost certainly other cases which have simply failed to be reported. Negative incidents of this type have in any case occurred in sufficient numbers to incite the insurance company Aegis London to propose an *ad hoc* contract, in the light of 'the very real risks hidden behind superyacht glamour'.

Chapter 7

The 'abode of production'

It is a curious study, as elusive as it is ambivalent. Indeed, only traces of it are to be found on line and not the document itself. At the beginning of 2013, a team from the London School of Economics (LSE), based on an unspecified department (though almost certainly the Department of Management) apparently submitted a report on the economic impact of superyachts, drawing on data from five countries over a five-year period. But submitted to whom? To the organization who had commissioned it, the Worldwide Yachting Association (which still used the acronym MYBA – the Mediterranean Yacht Broker Association – the name it was given when founded in 1984), an association with headquarters at Saint-Laurent-du-Var, in France. The choice of the LSE was clearly by no means a random one. This prestigious academic endorsement enabled them – as the secretary general of the association was quick to point out – to emphasize the serious nature of the organization and their determination to finally reach a 'neutral' and 'objective' conclusion, which would be a far cry from the misconceptions and damaging stereotypes that have clearly plagued the superyacht industry. Information versus malicious gossip, in a sense. This was all the more important in that, in reality, this was not simply a matter of bowing to the absolute impartiality of pure knowledge. On the contrary, the MYBA admitted on various occasions, this was about being able to apply pressure as leverage in their lobbying, notably in Brussels.

One of the possible ways of defining politics involves modifying social perceptions. What impact did it have? A mystery. But there must have been one, and it is quite possible that the effectiveness of the report was in inverse proportion to its visibility. In 2014, on the occasion of a celebration to mark its thirty years of existence, the MYBA listed this report, rubber stamped by the famous London university and described as a 'useful lobbying aid', as one of its thirty greatest successes.

With the global financial crisis, which began in 2007–8, rekindling the debate on inequalities, the strategy was to focus on prioritizing employment. Between 2007 and 2011, across all the European countries featured in the report (Spain, France, Greece, Italy and the Netherlands), the sector employed around 30,000 people. Even more impressively, it went against the tide of the prevailing economic downturn by taking on workers on a significant scale. But who exactly was being taken on? This is where the ambivalence of the strategy is in danger of an abrupt change of tack. For the vast majority of these new jobs primarily involved, and by a considerable margin, unskilled labour. The study concluded therefore that, in contrast to the 'glamour' image generally portrayed, a crucial aspect of this industry is in fact its 'hard-working physical labour force'. An aspect that is generally neglected, and even covered up, whereas in fact, as the study reveals, it represents 86.5% of the employment concerned.

What do we really know about this work? Virtually nothing. The data from the LSE's phantom study are extremely fragmented: of the 96 companies to whom the questionnaire was sent, only thirteen acknowledged receiving it, and, of these, only six or seven responded, the others taking refuge in the pretext of confidentiality. Employment is both celebrated and idealized. At the same time, in 2013 the president of another international superyachting association gleefully claimed that this sector was in fact the most ethical of any in the luxury world. His argument went like this: buying boats means creating jobs, buying very big boats means creating even more jobs. Why look for complications, when everything can be perfectly simple. The construction of a 65-meter yacht would, over a period of about two years, directly provide work for some 350 people. The average-sized shipyard employs between 500 and 700 people. But what about their status, their salary, their working conditions? All of that remains shrouded in the mist. It is far easier to obtain information about shipbuilders, architects, designers, decorators – all those whose mission is to render the useless desirable – than about the shipyard workers. The unions who represent them could no doubt provide some elements of a response, but the media could hardly be said to be exactly awash with their communications.

There is, however, no shortage of 'insider' descriptions of gala evenings from the world of superyachting. Indeed, such accounts regularly feature in the media associated with the business world and the luxury sector, thanks to reporters who have specialized in following the adventures of the well-to-do. With photos to prove it, one of them eagerly boasts about her gala evening at the Monaco Yacht Show in 2019, to which she had been fortunate enough to secure an invitation. The event involved the equivalent of 4.3 billion dollars' worth of boats (a record), moored for the occasion in Port Hercules, and an inaugural gala for 350 VIP guests, carefully selected (and usually well known to each other). She describes in lavish detail the flawless elegance of the guests, the presentation ceremony for four awards, quickly dispatched in the space of barely twenty minutes, so as to make time for the party and the unlimited top-end buffet . . . An eye-witness account of a party for the extremely wealthy, which ended demurely, well before midnight. An ostentatious form of reclusion of which we shall see similar examples later. Other coverage also features 'day in the life' accounts, press articles or enlightening videos focusing on a business leader, a designer or even a client, hiring a superyacht for a day for their personal delectation. But, when it comes to the places where these vessels are built, and to the lives of the men and women involved in their construction, it is a very different story . . .

Of course, none of this is exclusively associated with this sector. It is difficult not to be reminded of research carried out by French sociologists Stéphane Beaud and Michel Pialoux, who, at the end of the last century, looked back at working conditions over a ten-year period within a factory setting. Taking as their starting point the gap between the physical presence and the symbolic absence of the working class, they turned the spotlight on what was happening inside the factory walls – in this case a car manufacturing plant. More broadly, it is in the very nature of market ideology to conceal the social relations of production and the disguised conditions of extortion governing them. One of the most famous passages in Karl Marx's *Capital* highlighted the need to get away from the superficial and noisy sphere of exchange, consumption and circulation in order to penetrate the 'hidden abode of production', that secret place that conceals the mystery of surplus-value. The more opulence flaunts itself on the open stage, the more hidden that place seems to be.

Chapter 8

Amsterdam's Red Party

Whether you have visited me or not, you probably already know me by reputation, with my canals, my museums, my crooked houses, or else – the low-life version – my coffee-shops, my red-light district or my Lieverdje statue, a rallying point, and then a memorial, to the anti-establishment *Provos* in the mid 1960s. But, did you know, that every year, in one of my largest exhibition centres, I host the Global Superyacht Forum, one of the main events of its type, leaving aside the fireworks and the flamboyant spectacle that is the Monaco Yacht Show? Well, I am only passing on what my promotors say, but everything indicates this is the big deal.

When it first started, in 1993 (then known as 'Project 93'), it was a much more modest affair; at that time there were only about 1,500 superyachts in the world and there was no sign of the fourfold increase that would occur over a period of less than thirty years. The reality is that, since then, the whole thing has started to gain momentum and it has now become an unmissable event. For the space of a few days, I represent the world capital of the luxury yacht industry, since the organizers of the forum take advantage of the neighbouring presence of *Metstrade*, the largest trade exhibition of marine equipment. An opportunity for visitors to kill two birds with one stone.

From what I can see, 'forum' is nothing more than a slightly intellectual-chic term for a proper large-scale symposium. In other words, an event which, over three or four days, brings together several hundred delegates (if the current upward trend continues, the threshold of a thousand will soon be crossed) coming from thirty or so different countries. 'Developed' countries, of course. The participants are wide-ranging: representatives of boat-building firms and management companies, individual owners and managers, shipowners, brokers and consultants . . . And as many potential buyers as possible. It is all about giving these the maximum amount of space. People are there to gather information, of course, but above all to do business. Each year there is a different theme, such as the recent one devoted to *The Perfect Customer Journey*. In 2019, the forum was spread over three days with the first day focused on business, the second on owners and the third on technology. Already in 2017, a whole day was entirely set aside for 'technology' (and you should see what people include under this term).

Whether forum or symposium, by definition, this is an event where people talk to each other. Whether in the keynote session, in the workshops, in groups or face-to-face, openly or discreetly, in the middle of the room or in the corridors, looking each other in the eye or with their faces bent over their smartphones, officially or informally, over breakfast or dinner, people talk endlessly. About luxury yachting in all its aspects, from the most practical to the most abstract: materials, regulations, markets, taxes, design, construction, etc. And, naturally, they talk figures, a lot of them. Not surprisingly, the event tends to be rather gendered: in spite of a growing feminization of the sector, few women feature in the list of speakers.

As for the atmosphere, the entire event can be neatly summed up by the franglais word – *networking*.

The Social Activity and VIP Hospitality

Our Superyacht Events team is renowned for delivering social events that are fresh, informal, dynamic and fun, and our plans for The Superyacht Forum will not disappoint. Private dinners, breakfasts, lunches and VIP parties will form the social backbone of the programme, but we would like to reassure you that there will be no black ties and no awards ceremonies, just good wine, good food and good contacts. As you register for The Superyacht Forum, you will be notified of invitations and opportunities to sign up for additional extra-curricular social activities, something that Amsterdam is renowned for too.

The Networking

The Superyacht Forum is structured around networking and maximizing the opportunity to meet the people that you need to meet in order to develop your ideas and your business. During our research into the evolution of The Superyacht Forum, there was an overwhelming response from our delegate sectors that the most valuable aspect of our events is the way we create powerful networking opportunities and connect our VIPs with the supply chain. This is through structured meetings, face to face networking, social interaction, private focus groups and venue mapping.

In other words, no excuse for boredom. The brochures are adamant, this is no place for solemnity. Any stuffiness in terms of style is firmly banished in favour of a relaxed elegance. *Business* but *fun*. As stated in the editorial for the 2015 event, in a move to recapture the magic of an atmosphere somewhat dimmed by the financial crisis: 'Putting the Fun in the Fundamentals'.

You may well be asking yourself what on earth this has to do with the red organization promised by the title of this chapter. I apologize for misleading you but, if you were hoping to encounter some Batavian communist delegation, you have come to the wrong place. The dangers of polysemy. This is not about a political party but about a party-party. Red Party is the name given to the celebrations on the final evening. Why red? Because it is organized in collaboration with the Red Ensign Group, responsible for British shipping registers. A group which takes its name from the colour of a flag dating from the beginning of the sixteenth century, first adopted by the royal navy and then, up until the present day, by the British merchant navy. Thanks to the British crown, the territory extends as far as Bermuda, to the Cayman Islands or to the Isle of Man. No socialist paradise on the horizon therefore – only some lucrative tax havens.

Chapter 9

ISF-IFI & Co.

If luxury yachting attracted a certain amount of media attention in France prior to the Covid-19 pandemic, this was largely thanks to a tax 'reform' – here we need to reinforce the quotation marks, put them in bold, make them flash. On 1 January 2018, farewell ISF (*impôt de solidarité sur la fortune* – wealth tax), and welcome IFI (*impôt sur la fortune immobilière* – tax on real estate) and its sidekick PFU (*prélèvement forfaitaire unique* – a flat rate tax). As its name implies, the new tax does not apply to personal assets (movables), whether on land like luxury cars, or at sea. Superyachts are therefore very much at the forefront of an unmistakable abandonment of any form of solidarity. The category of transferable securities in fact extends well beyond just these concrete signs of wealth, since it includes financial products – and this is perhaps the key issue. The fact remains that superyachts objectivize the injustice of a decision that, by excluding these mobile signs and symbols of opulence, eliminates from its field of application an amount estimated to be around three quarters of the former ISF. And that in a context where, as we have pointed out already, inequalities in terms of wealth depend even more on assets than on income levels.

All this represents a gift that is so huge, so flagrant, so clearly iniquitous that, even within the parliamentary majority, it did not go down well. It should be pointed out that this was not exactly helpful in any attempts to convince people that Emmanuel Macron was not acting in the interests of the wealthy. The general rapporteur of the finance committee within the National Assembly, Joël Giraud, a member of a small centrist, liberal political group and appointed by the presidential party, clearly felt it did not give a favourable impression. Superyachts are all about 'showing off' and are 'non-productive'. Something needed to be done. Negotiations took place. In agreeing to a compromise, the Finance Ministry stood its ground on the key aspects but was prepared to give way on some accompanying measures. The tax would not be re-imposed therefore, but there would be an additional tax on luxury goods. This would be in the form of an annual fee for francization and navigation, which would, in theory, be paid by any French owner of a yacht measuring more than thirty meters (it is therefore the higher criteria, rather than that of 24 meters, which is retained, thereby limiting its range) and/ or exceeding a certain power. For boats from outside France a passport fee would need to be paid. A case of compensating, of making a few peripheral changes . . . anything to save face.

Or not.

'Reform of the ISF: the failure of the yacht tax' (*Les Échos*, 19 July 2018)

'Reform of the ISF: the 'yacht tax' brings in peanuts' (*Capital*, 19 July 2018)

'Taxes on yachts and luxury cars bring in precious little' (*Le Figaro*, 27–8 July 2019)

'The fiasco of the yacht tax'/ 'Yacht tax: the story of a fiscal shipwreck' (*Le Monde*, 8–9 September 2019)

'Who sunk the yacht tax?' (*Aujourd'hui en France*, 26 September 2019)

Not surprisingly, the defeat was a crushing one. The short-fall was so dramatic that the business press, not renowned for mockery, went to town over the flop. In the summers of 2018 and 2019, in other words respectively roughly six months and eighteen months after the measure approved in 2017 was introduced, calculations revealed that the increase in taxes had brought in around 85,000 euros over two consecutive years, whereas budget estimates were reported to be of the order of ten million euros – a hundred times more (enough to buy a superyacht, one journalist familiar with the going rates jok-ingly suggested). The origin of this latter figure is not very clear. Initially attributed to those within the Finance Ministry, who quickly denied any responsibility, it then appeared to have come from the president of the majority parliamentary group. In any case, there was something of a difference. At the start of the new political season in autumn 2019, the amount had indeed tripled, reaching 288,000 euros, but it still remained considerably lower than predicted. Furthermore, the two organizations most likely to reap any benefits – the Société nationale de sauvetage en mer and the Conservatoire du lit-toral (Coastal protection agency) – stated that they had not yet seen the colour of the money.

You are probably thinking that you would have to be naive to be surprised by any of this, but the general rapporteur of the finance committee was apparently taken aback. He strug-gled to understand the sums in question, not only in terms of quantity given how low they were, but also qualitatively, given the random nature of the decisions behind them. He was amazed to find that the customs authorities appeared to be conspicuously unforthcoming on the subject, as he discovered when paying them a short visit, on which occasion he learned that, first of all, the software programme was not really being used or updated and, secondly, that not a single customs check had been carried out in the Saint-Tropez area, clearly a key location in this context. He seemed so genuinely surprised that it was almost tempting to applaud his performance. For the fiasco is clearly not one at all, in the sense that it is by no means accidental but rather the consequence of a policy.

The budget rapporteur for the National Assembly appeared to have no idea about what he was getting into. Yet it is perfectly simple. In the course of an initial analysis of the first budgetary period, the *Observatoire français des conjonctures économiques* (the *OFCE* – French Economic Observatory) concluded that the re-distributional impact broadly favoured the 2% of households with the highest incomes, in other words, those who hold the majority of movable assets. The more modest households, in contrast, were severely affected, to their detriment of course, by the rise in indirect taxation. Three similar tax years brought little change: between 2018 and 2020 the richest were the biggest winners, the poorest the biggest losers. The standard of living of the 5% of French people on the lowest incomes continued to fall whereas that of the wealthiest 5% increased. In October 2019, the first report of a Capital Tax Reform Evaluation Committee failed to come up with a proper assessment (in fact it kicked the issue into the long grass), but the 'only concrete conclusion' to emerge, as journalist Romaric Godin wrote, is, 'as predicted', the increase in wealth of the richest 5%. Even *Le Monde*, not exactly at the cutting edge in the battle against neoliberalism and grudgingly, and wrongly, (dis)qualifying the OFCE as 'a left-leaning think tank' (it is in fact a publicly funded research centre in economics housed at Sciences Po), was nevertheless forced to agree that it was indeed the richest who stood to gain from the 'reforms'. According to calculations made by the *Institut des politiques publiques* for the years 2018–19, it was the wealthiest 1%, and even more, 0.1% who came off best. One thing is certain beyond these variations: the poorest are the ones footing the bill.

All perfectly normal. It was not just the fiscal policy but the entire economic policy of the elected government, which, well beyond the matter of conversion from ISF to IFI, favours wealth. It could even be described as a transfer of resources to the wealthiest, resulting in a budgetary loss for the state. An anti-redistributive or, put better, counter-redistributive policy, in other words one that distributes in the wrong direction, like a head-over-heels Robin Hood. Looking at the situation in France and around the world, Attac and the Copernic Foundation do indeed observe a movement, but one going from the bottom towards the top. 'More than just a trickle, it is a torrent which carries everything towards the richest people.' Given this is not likely to be the preferred reading of a budget rapporteur, let us provide him with a further extract: 'Never has a government of the Fifth Republic previously dared to put in place a tax policy so clearly in favour of the rich and of finance.' That clarifies matters, does it not? The fact that the rich are becoming richer, on the other hand, has been repeatedly confirmed on numerous fronts, from INSEE (the National Institute of Statistics and Economic Studies) to the very official institution *France Stratégie*, under the aegis of the Prime Minister.

No need incidentally to wait for the ISF to be replaced by the IFI, or the equivalent foreign regulations, to start evading tax constraints. Quite clearly, where there is taxation, there is tax fraud – 'fiscal optimization', for anyone with a little *savoir-vivre* and a knowledge of the law. By definition, boats can easily take advantage of their mobility to flee compromising situations. Taking this logic to its limit, some of them remain at sea all year long: no registration, no taxes. Not only are superyachts registered in *offshore* locations and make frequent stopovers there, but they are themselves floating tax havens. (It can never be emphasized enough what a master stroke lay behind the misleading term 'haven', given that for the majority of people, 'hell' would be a more appropriate word.) Superyacht owners are all too well aware that white-collar crime in general, and tax crime in particular, are very far from being a political priority.

They may not be in the habit of reading works of social science but they have a practical sense of tax impunity. Some of them are even masters of the art. Bernard Tapie, for example, who hired out his superyacht *Reborn* (alias *Bodicea*), flying the flag of the Isle of Man, for around 600,000 euros a week. The boat was acquired with part of the windfall from the Adidas case, a highly controversial outcome and therefore public money – more than 400 million euros generously financed by tax payers. And telecommunications magnate Xavier Niel, owner of *Phocéa*, another boat previously owned by the very same Bernard Tapie, is known to hate sailing, a fact that suggests that his purchase was scarcely motivated by a love of the sea.

A love of islands, on the other hand . . . the vessel is registered in Malta, a key location within the European Union, and a direct competitor with the British network. For those not in the know, whether genuinely or not, the *Malta Files* along with the *Paradise Papers* lifted the curtain on some of the strategies deployed to avoid or reduce fiscal liability, in whatever form, from wealth tax, fuel tax or VAT. In order to make VAT less painful you can for example, by means of a well-established set-up, charter out your yacht to yourself or even pass it off as a cruise ship or a commercial vessel. Furthermore, the 'flexibility' of employment law, as it is described by those working hard to destroy it, and the low level of social security contributions in Malta – with cut-price unemployment rights and retirement rights on the cheap – have made the 'Maltese contract' famous, including in the case of staff employed from France and Italy. The milestone whereby people have been blackmailed into relocating has long been passed.

A superyacht is certainly versatile. A mobile income thanks to chartering, it can serve as a hiding place where necessary, for example for valuable goods from a dubious provenance (not long ago, one collector affirmed that it was indeed the Superyacht *Serene* that provided a hiding place for the elusive painting 'Salvator Mundi' attributed to Leonardo da Vinci and reputed to be the most expensive work of art in the world), or for suspect practices such as a thinly disguised form of pimping, rarely identified as such, or it can itself serve as a money laundering mechanism. Nothing illustrates this better than the so called '1MDB' affair, named after a Malaysian investment fund, which provoked an international financial scandal featuring at its heart the aptly named *Equanimity*, all marble and gilt and flying the flag of the Cayman Islands. With an estimated value of 250 million dollars, it was seized in 2018 by the Malaysian government, at the request of the American authorities, in an enormous money laundering operation involving several countries (bank accounts in Singapore, the USA and in Switzerland). It was a convoluted affair with multiple ramifications, which demonstrates that, far from being in clear opposition to each other, legality and illegality are in fact interwoven. Once the case had been put to rest, *Equanimity* was renamed – no joke here – *Tranquility*. No doubt the taxpaying citizens appreciated this change of name, reminiscent of the all-too famous dictum that the bigger the lie, the better it works.

Chapter 10

Riding the (financial) storm

'The luxury yachting sector is not affected by the crisis' claimed geographers Michel Desse and Simon Charrier ten years on from the start of the subprime crisis. In spite of a slight downturn or slow down, this was still 'a thriving economic sector', as demonstrated first of all by the ever-growing numbers of superyachts in use throughout the world over the course of the last few decades.

Let us look more closely at the situation in order to paint a fairer picture. Looked at through a magnifying glass, there was indeed something of a critical phase. Anxiety among actors within the industry surged at the beginning of 2010. There was even, for a while, a hint of fear in the air. Code name, GFC – global financial crisis. Objectively, such feelings were based on a number of specific elements. Hasty resales (like that of Martin Bouygues, who apparently got rid of *Bâton Rouge*, 62 meters long, only two years after commissioning it), boats not selling or even impossible to sell, the downward trend in certain sale prices, the seizing-up of the crewed charter market, small companies going under, even attempts at insurance fraud as a way of getting rid of a plaything that had begun to prove something of a burden. The construction boom stagnated and order numbers plummeted. Ten years after the start of the crisis, the number of deliveries barely reached the maximum level for the years 2006–8, when it averaged around 250 per year. Yet the effect of all this was not evenly felt. The lowest end of the sector, relatively speaking, found itself most affected by the impact, whereas the market for vessels in excess of sixty to seventy meters still continued to thrive. An unsinkable micro-market niche sheltered from economic fluctuations.

It is clear that the term 'crisis', already considerably over-used, is rather too big a word for what we are looking at here, which could perhaps be more appropriately described as a minor slump. In 2012, there were fears for Bernard Arnault, who, four years earlier, had bought two shipyards specializing in very high-end products; however, to everyone's relief, he bounced back and has since overtaken Bill Gates on the podium of the world's wealthiest individuals, as ranked by Bloomberg. Overall, the crisis faded quickly. Business as usual was resumed, with certain peripheral adaptations, visible only to specialists, like the increased importance of the larger-scale constructors. Even in the midst of the so-called crisis many encouraging signs could be spotted, ranging from the opening of Porto Montenegro in 2009 to the construction of *Azzam* in 2013. All in all, the effects appear to have been both modest and short-lived.

The industry emerged even stronger, having rapidly over-come this crisis. 'Resilience' was, rightly or wrongly (wrongly, more often than not), on everyone's lips and rarely has a word found such favour so fast. Even here, there was no escaping it. In 2016, a report entitled *The State of Wealth, Luxury and Yachting*, compiled by two companies based respectively in New York and in London, found no evidence of any resultant damage. From 2014 onwards, it was all systems go once again and, at the end of the following year, specialists were congratulating themselves on their excellent results. That year saw order numbers overtaking deliveries by a small margin. The number of new constructions exceeding the (not only) symbolic figure of one hundred meters also reached record levels. Acting as a kind of bible for the sector, though somewhat less venerable (it was first created in 1992), the *Global Order Book* provides solid evidence that transactions were extremely healthy, with 773 superyachts ordered or under construction in 2018, and 830 in 2019.

All in all, with the exception of a peak in 2008–9, at the height of the financial crisis, figures relating to construction were more or less stable and, a decade later, the order books were looking full. In the medium term, the spectacular boom in the worldwide luxury yacht industry is unmistakable. The number of superyachts has increased sixfold since 1985, having crossed the threshold of a thousand units at the beginning of the 1970s; and this number has shown no decline year on year, with projections continuing to rise. The dynamics of the lavish one-upmanship associated with the yachting activities of the world's wealthiest individuals show no signs of slowing down. Far from it.

Year	Number of superyachts
1985	809
1986	859
1987	917
1988	966
1989	1052
1990	1090
1991	1169
1992	1238
1993	1305
1994	1370
1995	1429
1996	1485
1997	1557
1998	1643

Year	Number of superyachts
1999	1731
2000	1835
2001	1952
2002	2093
2003	2240
2004	2411
2005	2577
2006	2793
2007	3031
2008	3290
2009	3507
2010	3716
2011	3891
2012	4083
2013	4254
2014	4404
2015	4547
2016	4704
2017	4851
2018	4950
2019	5096
2020	5245

'Meanwhile, this much is clear', wrote journalist Giles Whittell in 2019, referring with approval to what might be described as a resurrection in an industry which has been severely tested: 'when the history of the past decade comes to be written, the survival of superyachts will deserve a part in it'. In a sense, it is difficult to disagree with him entirely.

Of course, specialists within the sector take a somewhat cautious line. Not wishing to cry victory, they depict the super-yacht market as young, tentative and immature. Those involved, they predict, need to learn from the more long-established luxury markets, with more mature growth curves. They regret that progress has not been quite as spectacular as predicted, given the hopes raised by the boom at the turn of the century, at the time when the threshold of two thousand vessels had been crossed and, again, when it looked as though the doubling in size of the fleet between the beginning of the 2000s and the start of the following decade might be reproduced. Retrospectively and prospectively, the *Superyacht Industry Manifesto* already cited takes a restrained stance. Progress is satisfactory, without being excessive. In the midst of chaos, better to remain cautious.

Imagine, just for one moment, what would happen if there was a pandemic . . . Well, even in this case, chaos could indeed prove to be profitable. In summer 2020, a report on the state of billionaires' wealth, co-signed by the UBS bank and the consultants PricewaterhouseCoopers and entitled 'Riding the Storm', indicates that they have come out of the situation extremely well, in particular when they chose to invest in new technologies. Their accrued wealth has never looked so healthy. The cover of the report, showing the prow of a ship about to be engulfed by the waves, is therefore somewhat misleading. In view of the climate of instability, some of those within the sector have taken to philosophizing, with the touching clumsiness of those not in the habit of doing so:

> 'There's a wonderful quote from Charles Darwin that I've adapted slightly; "it's not the strongest in the superyacht market that survive, it's those most adaptable or responsive to change" '. [. . .]
>
> 'I find it hard to contemplate how the world will behave after COVID-19. Perhaps mankind will think more philosophically and intelligently about what they need or how they behave. It may take longer than we all think for the aftermath to add up and return to the new normal. Or once it's all over, we will breathe a huge sigh of relief and go back to the way we were, becoming conspicuous consumers of anything and everything

we don't need. To be honest, this keeps me awake at night, trying to contemplate what is on the superyacht horizon.'

Since then, that horizon has remained perfectly clear: the superyachting industry is doing very well. Probably even better than ever. Now is the 'greatest boom in the yacht business that's ever existed', an industry professional told reporter Evan Osnos in a 2022 *New Yorker* article as extensive as it was edifying. Even a former CIA officer, quoted in the same piece, sees a 'Faustian capitalism' at work in superyachts, in which democracy is sold for short-term profit.

Chapter 11

Conspicuous seclusion

Making an impression while keeping away from prying eyes. Showing off and staying hidden. Not as contradictory as it might seem. Like distinction and imitation, rather than excluding each other, visibility and invisibility are mutually supportive.

First and foremost, it is all about visibility – and with good reason. Clearly, the superyacht is there to attract attention. Its physical presence is not designed with subtlety in mind, especially given the frantic drive for ever-increasing length. A glaring expression of the lifestyle of those referred to both in international academic literature and in everyday language as the 'super-rich' or 'ultra-rich', the practice of luxury yachting is the ultimate marker of social distinction. The use – and in particular ownership – of a superyacht constitutes one of the most obvious and substantial exterior signs of wealth – the very opposite of a fortune rendered abstract by its diffusion into intangible financial assets. As proof that visibility takes precedence over utility, owners are quick to tire of their possessions and generally get rid of their costly playthings less than three years after acquiring them, as though these sophisticated constructions, these gems of engineering, rapidly became obsolete. As a matter of fact, most superyachts have lost part of their value by the time they are resold. In investment terms, as even *The Financial Times* admits, 'a superyacht is a terrible asset'.

It is tempting, in this respect, to interpret the practice of superyachting on the basis of categories devised at the end of the nineteenth century by Thorstein Veblen in his book 'The Theory of the Leisure Class' ('"idle class" would have done just as well', as the book's French translator suggested). These categories include those of 'conspicuous leisure' and of 'conspicuous consumption' following on, in his book, from that of 'pecuniary emulation'. The American sociologist saw these as different aspects of a process of emulation, freed from any strictly utilitarian calculation or from the presence of any real needs to be satisfied, and sometimes leading to what he refers to as 'conspicuous wastefulness'. What counts above all is the demonstration of a social superiority. 'In order to gain and to hold the esteem of men it is not sufficient merely to possess wealth or power. The wealth or power must be put in evidence, for esteem is awarded only on evidence. And not only does the evidence of wealth serve to impress one's importance on others and to keep their sense of his importance alive and alert, but it is scarcely less use in building up and preserving one's self-complacency.'

Times have changed, of course, with the decline of the aristocratic ethos. The idle class of the past made a show of the fact that they had sufficient leisure to devote themselves, in a sense freely, without the necessity for any economic motive, to occupations that, although not necessarily extravagant in themselves (such as a taste for politics or for sport for example) were free from the constraints of any productive work. A century later, even if wealth is predominantly inherited, the wealthiest individuals never miss an opportunity to extol the invaluable virtues of 'work' (even going so far as to describe the superyacht itself as a work space, where for example, contracts can be negotiated and signed), in a way that turns leisure into a just reward for duty, rather than the fruit of earlier achievements. The forms of what Veblen terms 'honorific waste', the environmental costs of which he was among the first to identify, have therefore changed somewhat, but the need to display, or even to show off, still remains.

Display therefore, but just as importantly, retreat. As well as a flagrant physical presence, the superyacht is also an enclosed space, a place of seclusion. Ships had their place in the typology of total institutions described by Erving Goffman in his book *Asylums*. For Goffman, they belonged to a category devoted to some instrumental purpose, whether education or work – the merchant navy typically – but we could also refer here to another of his categories, in which he placed convents and monasteries, places of voluntary retreat from the world. For the superyacht is also, somewhat prosaically, precisely that: the physical guarantee of a private space, the assurance of a tightly defined security. It is, in this sense, closely akin to the gated community, a residential community closed off almost as though under siege conditions, rather than to an ordinary vessel or a densely populated cruise ship. A spatial seclusion on a reduced scale amounting to a social withdrawal on a grand scale, a sort of detachment in the form of an exit on the part of the elite, the archetype of which, perfectly compatible with the superyacht, is the libertarian dream of an island for wealthy individuals free from all state control. A state of isolation, which cuts the individuals concerned off from a certain world rather than from the world in general, and one which is in fact entirely relative given its reliance on networks providing long-distance connections. The myth of self-sufficiency nevertheless continues to thrive. There are even two vessels, named respectively *Mirage* and *Hide*, which, by means of an arrangement of mirrors, are designed to become almost invisible.

Difficult therefore to avoid resorting to an oxymoron in

MAIN DECK

LOWER DECK

Figure 2 Hide yacht (49.9 m) © Anna Borla Design & Yachts

order to express in the shortest possible way this underlying tension between display and retreat, between putting yourself on show and hiding away. Hence 'conspicuous seclusion'. The term implies forms of retreat that are paradoxically designed to attract attention. Think of private, chauffeur-driven cars, usually black vehicles, equipped with tinted windows, making it impossible to see inside, but which are unmistakable from the outside, particularly when driven along leafy highways.

Think also, in a more open way, of those expensive beach clubs where space is heavily commercialized. While these are separated from the free sections of the beaches by permanent structures and wooden barriers emphasizing socio-spatial segregation, these establishments with their extensive restaurant facilities allow 'ordinary' bathers a view of the sumptuous tables and even more of the deck-chairs and loungers, 'VIP beds' included. But superyachts unmistakably epitomize this conspicuous seclusion. Their extravagant external dimensions inevitably attract attention, but are designed to keep the internal spaces and, in particular, what goes on behind the scenes, well concealed from prying eyes.

This falsely contradictory logic illustrates the way in which the superior classes control their visibility, both in terms of their own class and of others, in order to establish a balance between being on show and conserving privacy. While it is true that globalization tends to come at the price of isolation, it is not only the poorest people who are affected by this. It also manifests itself at the summit of the social pyramid, though, in the very different form of chosen seclusion rather than imposed captivity. This capacity to show yourself or not, to choose only to reveal yourself when among peers, is one facet of the power exercised by the dominant classes over time and space and, by extension, of their power in general.

Here, as elsewhere, the Covid-19 pandemic proved enlightening. In 2020, David Geffen, the very wealthy producer, sparked a minor outburst of fury on social and digital networks after using one of these to share the photo of a sunset taken from his secluded Caribbean isolation on board *Rising Sun*, under the pretence of voicing concern for other people's state of health. Nor was he alone, for, in spite of a few minor inconveniences, which were inevitable given the situation, the pandemic transformed superyachts, along with private jets used to ferry people to their isolated places of residence, into desirable retreats. It seems likely that this combination of survivalism and separatism as understood by the wealthiest individuals has a bright future and – all things considered – a superyacht is considerably more comfortable than a bunker, no matter how well-equipped it may be. The ship may well be the 'heterotopia *par excellence*' that Michel Foucault once spoke of.

Chapter 12

The political geography of luxury sailing

Traditionally the geography of superyachting is governed by two main centres of attraction. Adopting an expression originally coined in war logistics, the name 'milk run' is given to the practice of transiting from one to the other according to a well-established itinerary and a seasonal and fashionable transatlantic calendar.

The summer centre (from April to September) is concentrated on the Mediterranean. About two-thirds of the total global fleet pass through here. More specifically, through an area enclosed within what is sometimes referred to as the golden triangle, between the Côte d'Azur, alias the French Riviera (key location: Saint-Tropez), the Gulf of Genoa, alias the Italian Riviera (key location: Portofino), and Sardinia (key location: Porto Cervo). In a more restricted interpretation, the term 'milk run' sometimes refers only to a route leading from Saint-Tropez to Porto Cervo via Monaco (and Port Hercules), Antibes (and Port Vauban, along with Camille-Rayon Quay, otherwise known as 'billionaires quay'), and the Cannes and Nice region, Saint-Jean-Cap-Ferrat, Golfe-Juan, Corsica, and then, in Italy, the bay of Naples and the Amalfi coast. More recently, the centre of gravity has shifted to the west, with the increased popularity of the Balearic Islands (key locations: Palma de Majorca and Ibiza); in addition, to the north, the Catalan coast (notably Port Vell in Barcelona, constructed for the 1992 Olympic Games) and to the south the Costa del Sol around Marbella, with Valence between the two.

The winter centre (still from the perspective of the northern hemisphere) is concentrated around the Caribbean. This zone stretches from south of Florida (key locations: Fort Lauderdale, to the north of Miami, and the island of Palm Beach), as far as the islands of Grenada and Barbados, via the Bahamas Archipelago, Saint Martin and Saint-Barthelemy (or Saint Barts). To the north, the Bermudas (apparently without the effects of the famous triangle) and to the west Cancún on the entrance to the Gulf of Mexico. Quite a turnaround, since at the beginning of the eighteenth century, following the emergence of buccaneering, the Caribbean became a favoured haunt for Atlantic piracy in its golden age. Made up of impoverished sailors fleeing the drudgery that was their lot, this band of brothers set out to organize power in a democratic manner and to share their spoils fairly, as we learn from the lively account of historian Marcus Rediker. Less than three centuries later, this area provides shelter for the luxury vessels belonging to a handful of billionaires embracing absolutely contrary values but, in their case, avoiding the stigma of criminal status.

Over the course of the last few years, however, there have been signs that these areas are being demoted in favour of newly emerging destinations, now extremely attractive and therefore strong competitors, since they tend to be less crowded, less expensive and more exotic. This is the case for Eastern Europe, the entire Adriatic coast, Croatia (where in 2020 rapper Jay-Z and singer Beyoncé chose to take up residence on board the luxury yacht *Lana* – 1.7 million dollars minimum per week for rental alone) and as far as Montenegro, and particularly Porto Montenegro, situated on a former Yugoslavian naval base. In Greece, after the majority of the country's population had suffered the full brunt of the economic persecution imposed at the hands of the Troika, prices dropped and several bays and islands are once again popular with the most affluent. A general trend can also be observed towards the Indian Ocean, sparked by the construction of huge marinas in the Gulf of Oman and the Persian Gulf and centred around Dubai, Abu Dhabi and also Kuwait, Bahrain, Qatar and the Maldives.

To a lesser extent, attention is also beginning to be directed towards Russia (a constructor has taken advantage of a marina built under the aegis of Stalin on the Moscow River to attract local oligarchs) as well as Brazil, and even India, following the lead of the billionaire Lakshmi Mittal, owner of *Amevi*, acquired in 2007 for 140 million euros and chartered for 700,000 euros per week. Since the turn of the century, even China has entered the race with the construction of quays capable of accommodating superyachts, particularly at Haikou, an island situated on the north coast of Hainan and sometimes referred to as the 'Chinese Hawaii'. There are plans to open dozens, perhaps even hundreds, of marinas there, even though the popularity of luxury yachts still remains extremely uncertain. Otherwise, rather than simply basking in the sun, there is a growing 'trend' to venture as far as Greenland (or at the opposite pole, the Antarctic), driven by a burgeoning taste for these expeditions, which not only require vessels equipped with ice-breakers but also mean considerably higher fuel costs.

On the back of a movement that has now spread to the four corners of the globe, Australia is making its presence felt more and more visibly on the superyachting world map. Without being an isolated case, its presence there allows us to speak in terms of a political geography. Governmental involvement to encourage economic appeal has been particularly evident here. Following publication of a report on the economic potential of this sector in 2017, which succeeded in whetting certain appetites, a five-year plan was put in place in order to facilitate, both in physical and fiscal terms, the arrival of large vessels.

Its objective was to push the local economic impact, recently estimated at less than two billion Australian dollars, to a figure in excess of the three billion mark. It would after all be a pity to allow all of that to slip into the hands of New Zealand, the Fiji Islands or Tahiti. In the interests of saving jobs, you understand.

In this context, there is no need to go so far afield in order to uncover some surprises. It is unlikely that French singer-songwriter Georges Brassens would still insist on being buried on the beach at Sète, given that the Occitania municipality has in recent years announced plans to develop the port so as to create capacity for superyachts and to organize an entire industry based on them. These plans have met with local opposition based on a combination of social, economic and ecological reasons. In 2017, a USA/United Arab Emirates consortium was chosen by the president of the Sète management committee. But who exactly is this staunch advocate for the arrival of luxury yachts, waging a powerful battle, in the name of development, against local people in heated meetings, in the course of which Monaco and Saint-Tropez are unfavourably cited? None other than the former deputy of Seine-Saint-Denis and Minister for Public Works, Transport and Housing at the time of the 'gauche plurielle' (the plural left, a left-wing coalition in France from 1997 until 2002): the communist Jean-Claude Gayssot. (To be fair, he also declared himself ready to welcome Aquarius, the humanitarian vessel rescuing migrants at sea.)

The Mediterranean must rid itself of the still-lingering spectre of decline. For the time being, contrary to many predictions, it has succeeded in doing so. In 2019, in response to the question 'Monaco and the Côte d'Azur: Are They the Global Superyacht Capitals?', The Superyacht Business Report replied in the affirmative. A number of threats clearly still exist, including the recently declared intention by the French authorities to introduce stricter (and, one might say from another perspective, more reasonable) environmental regulations. This, nevertheless, fails to alter the fact that, for reasons that are as much symbolic as material and that involve a combination of the existing highly efficient infrastructures and an unrivalled reputation as a fashionable location, this status persists. If changes have indeed taken place (the specialist adds), these have certainly been exaggerated – strongholds endure.

So much for routes. For the map changes dramatically if we focus on a different aspect. Swap destination for construction and one country – Italy – far outstrips any others. In 2018, 'the Boot' as it is sometimes called, accounted for almost half of current constructions, well ahead of the Netherlands and Germany, countries highly regarded within the top end of the market. That year, the biggest transalpine constructors (Azimut-Benetti, Ferretti, Sanlorenzo) even monopolized the world podium. It is true that some countries, such as Turkey, where wages are still lower than elsewhere, are rapidly catching up and, conversely, that American constructors saw their share of the market drop steeply after 2010. But the USA has nevertheless made up for that fall when it comes to ownership. In the middle of the last decade, it was estimated that around a third of superyacht owners were American, a much greater proportion than either the British or the Russians. That being said, it all depends on where exactly the cursor is placed; narrow it down to the one hundred largest superyachts, and that third shifts to those originating from Arabic countries: Oman, Saudi Arabia and Egypt. Destination, construction, ownership – so many different criteria, so many different maps. Superimpose the flows of production and of consumption in the context of superyachting and one of the faces of global capitalism is revealed.

Chapter 13

Playing the eco-friendly card (greenwashing)

It goes without saying that the different forms of sailing, from the humblest to the most luxurious, mirror socio-economic inequalities. What is perhaps less obvious is that this physical dimension also brings with it a warped symbolic dimension. Social perception of the activity of sailing is indeed permeated by a powerful class inequality. Taking the case of Marseille as his starting point, sociologist Jean-Louis Fabiani observed that paradoxically, perhaps even illogically, sailing activities associated with the working classes tended to be more severely stigmatized for the pollution they caused than was the case with bourgeois sailing activities, 'regarded as an ecological sport, which relies solely on renewable resources and gives rise to a whole range of aesthetic sensations'. And that is in spite of the fact that the carbon footprint of the very large vessels, an indicator that is admittedly at best only a partial one, is out of all proportion to that of more modest examples.

Fabiani situates this state of affairs within the context of 'the long history of the subjugation of the working classes'; a history of the moral, if not legal, condemnation of their activities. In this particular case, in contrast with the presumed aesthetic tastes and ecological preoccupations of the upper classes, the most inoffensive, or least harmful activity is reduced to something distasteful – a contrast between what is worthy of being liked and what is to be disliked, which is essentially that between right and wrong. The aura conferred on the most inveterate polluters by an undeserved presumption of ecological concern ends up turning things upside down. Without any hint of shame, the opulent colossus described by *Paris Match* in 2018 as 'the craziest superyacht in the world' was christened *Nature*. 'Nature is often synonymous with perfection. And you are never closer to nature than on a yacht', as the founder of the specialized design studio responsible for the project unabashedly declares – for it is, at the moment, no more than simply a project.

Given that superyachts are not exactly known for being self-effacing, it is difficult to disguise their huge environmental impact. Certain practitioners have even inadvertently given the game away by vandalizing the environments they pass through, without exercising the required level of discretion. In February 2020, the owner of a hedge fund got caught red-handed because his yacht, *Samadhi* (a Buddhist term meaning meditative concentration and spiritual elevation) damaged an atoll in Belize, classified as a UNESCO world heritage site. Four years earlier, *Tatoosh*, owned by businessman Paul Allen, caused serious damage to 1,300 square meters of coral reef in the Cayman Islands; if even tax havens are no longer respected, what hope is there?

By the very fact that it involves the movement of large-scale vessels, which are usually motor powered (that is the case for around 80–85% of the world fleet), luxury sailing is intrinsically an activity that generates pollution. First of all, there is the pollution produced by the boats themselves, ranging from exhaust emissions (a full tank amounts to tens, even hundreds, of thousands of litres of diesel), to the use of antifouling paints containing toxic substances, or sacrificial anodes placed below the flotation line in order to reduce the corrosion of metal parts. Then there is the pollution caused by the behaviour of those on board, including disposal of waste water, rubbish and detergents. Not to mention the disturbance to ecosystems resulting from noise, vibration and artificial lighting, but also, as we shall discover later in this book, from the practices associated with mooring and the effects this has on the seabed. And, even before any pollution directly associated with the use of these vessels, there is also the damage caused by the extraction of materials used in their construction, including those that are wrongly regarded as being inexhaustible, such as sand.

A group of four American academics, who set out to measure the environmental damage caused by the excessive consumption of luxury commodities, found themselves having to restrict their focus to the carbon footprint indicator, given the impossibility of taking all these parameters into account. A significant underestimation, therefore, which did, however, enable them to establish that, on average, a superyacht generates as much carbon dioxide as more than 200 American cars and that the total fleet of the 300 biggest superyachts in active use generates annual emissions of almost 630 million pounds (around 285,000 tons) of carbon dioxide, as much therefore, if not more, as many entire countries, such as Burundi. 'Legally, of course, conspicuous consumption is not a crime – it is an acceptable form of behavior encouraged under capitalism. But perhaps it should become a crime, given its adverse ecological impacts.' Did I hear someone say 'climaticide'?

As a result, spokespersons for the superyacht industry now find themselves constantly talking about environmental preoccupations. They, too, have been touched by the grace of 'sustainability'. They, too, must now play the ecological card – yet playing, as everyone knows, generally implies knowing how to trick or to bluff. For the idea of associating superyachts and restraint would, well, how should we put it . . . require a very well-honed sense of *greenwashing*. One of the major media groups within the industry therefore added a sustainability report to their portfolio, alongside sections on business or migration. The report appeared in number 200 of their publication, in 2020, complete with neat, nicely rounded figures. The *'Superyacht Industry Manifesto'*, which is also included, states that environmental and social commitment will arguably be decisive (let us not mince words) for the future of the industry, that, without giving up luxury (let's be reasonable), superyachts can indeed become a force for good – as simple as that.

> Perhaps the most significant characteristic of the latter 2010s was the booming interest in the global climate crisis and the environmental and social agenda. It should be noted that while interest has grown significantly, it is not yet ubiquitous. [. . .] The hypocrisy of professing to love the ocean and then actively polluting it no longer passes muster. [. . .] The need to be environmentally sustainable is only going to become greater. On the one hand, it will be driven by regulations and requirements; on the other, it will be influenced by consumer pressure. Therefore, in order to remain a viable pastime for the world's ultra-wealthy, the next ten years must be characterized by a shift towards alternative (green) fuels, alternative (sustainable) materials, reduced wastage, a reduction in single-use plastics and more. (*The Superyacht Industry Manifesto*, 2020)

Not exactly what could be described as a deeply rooted environmental conviction, devoid of any ulterior motives, therefore, but the expression of a clearly understood vested interest – the 'new generation' of super-rich individuals is by definition younger and young people are more concerned about the environmental situation – the conclusion of the syllogism makes perfect sense.

The result of all this is that media and publicity sources serving the luxury market are quick to present the industry as one determined to protect the environment. In at least one of the professional salons dedicated to design, there is now an *ad hoc* reward in the form of the Environmental Protection Award or, in its abbreviated form, Eco Award. The name of the game is all about reducing the carbon footprint. The principal means of achieving that goal involves adopting systems where hybrid propulsion, electricity or hydrogen take over from fossil fuels. But it also means installing solar panels, increasing the use of energy-saving electricity on board, introducing more energy-efficient air-conditioning systems and obtaining accreditation for any rare materials (including gold) that could potentially have a dubious provenance. Not to mention a little dose of philanthropy hastily greenwashed, involving participation in conservation programmes or even scientific exploration, since, after all, ecology is historically and conceptually first and foremost a science. In this respect, 2024 should see the launch of *REV* (*Research and Expedition Vessel*), a 182-meter vessel, belonging to a Norwegian billionaire, designed to enable forty or so scientists to conduct oceanographic research in a setting that is privileged in every sense of the word. The same card is being played by *Njord*, a project that has raised the stakes dramatically by announcing the 2024 launch of a private superyacht measuring more than 270 meters. Even before that happens, *The Economist*, the liberal-minded weekly publication, commented ironically that the next time you see a party in full swing on a superyacht, you should not be tempted to think that everyone is just having fun. It could be that those people are simply conducting an experiment in naval technology.

But let us, nevertheless, be a little more serious. Ecology is all very well, but you can have too much of a good thing. The industry needs to make itself heard in terms of environmental legislation – a little more loudly than others, if possible. This is the job of the International Council of Marine Industry Associations (ICOMIA). And no one can accuse them of prevarication. In fact, they make reading between the lines almost a waste of time.

The association makes no pretence to be anything other than what it is – a pressure group. Naturally, it makes every effort to draw attention to its determination to protect marine environments, even condemning, for good measure, short-term negligence. Regardless of what anyone may think, it is now scarcely possible to profess indifference on this subject. With the current focus on ecological awareness, even taking into account its diversity or its indeterminate nature, it has become difficult, even impossible, not to take it seriously. Yet rhetorical concession is short lived. The real spectre, the association goes on to explain, is not ecological, but judicial. 'Legislation hostile to the industry' – that is the enemy. For environmental legislation is all very well, but it is expensive: better to say – rhetoric once again – that jobs are threatened.

As proof of the effectiveness of its lobbying, the association vaunts its success in terms of the revision of the framework directive prepared by the European Union on industrial emissions. A satisfactory outcome was reached from the association's point of view, which succeeded in convincing the Commission to give shipyards themselves, that is to say the companies that control them, the responsibility for finding the right balance in terms of conformity with environmental regulations. Repression should give way to regulation and, better still, to self-regulation: 'leave us to get on with it, we are the professionals', urge the employers. But if it is good to react, it is even better to anticipate. And better still to de-escalate.

Traditional defensive lobbying protective of the status quo is often insufficient. Instead, a high degree of proactivity is required. This translates into industry involvement before a legislation is proposed by authorities, and that we are accepted as a competent stakeholder to represent as well as to support our industry in relation to the particular legislations. This proactivity often helped to prevent rules in their early stages.

In Europe this requires us to act on multiple levels:

1. Attending the European Commission Meetings at various tiers of decision making;
2. Nurturing a constructive relationship with the committees of the EU parliament in relation to the particular legislations and members of EU parliament (MEPs);
3. Maintaining good relationships with the permanent representatives of the member states of the EU Council;
4. Good coordination with the relevant sister/partner association(s).

In the context of a rise in 'potential legislative threats', the document goes on to identify ten priority issues, including legislation concerning timber and construction wood, the targets for reducing greenhouse gas emissions and, more broadly, all regulations concerning marine and coastal environments. It concludes with a strategic line as clear as it gets:

To prevent hostile legislation, efficient lobbying requires various levels of engagement. As much as this intends to do its utmost to counterbalance or even oppose the ever-increasing legislative pressure, it also involves being a trusted and proactive stakeholder showing solutions that mitigate negative impact.

Chapter 14

Posidonia

I am usually referred to as 'Posidonia seagrass'. Other names include Neptune grass or Mediterranean tapeweed but you can just call me 'Posidonia'. Or *Posidonia oceanica,* to use my scientific title. Named by Carl Linnaeus in person, one of the most famous botanists in history.

As I am not easy to chart, my ecology was initially somewhat sketchy. For a long time, the exact conditions of my reproduction remained shrouded in a certain amount of mystery. Any claim that I am now widely known would be something of an exaggeration. In terms of scientific knowledge, the situation has improved enormously over the course of the last decades but there is still much to be done when it comes to the general public. Even today I am easily – and wrongly – mistaken for a seaweed. Worse still, people often think (completely wrongly) that I am just useless rubbish. Luckily there are hard-working scientists and that helps to set things straight. Thanks to the work of an *ad hoc* French scientific interest group called 'GIS Posidonie', set up in 1982, and still active, I am now reasonably well understood.

Bearing no resemblance to a seaweed, I am a flowering plant. A species endemic to the Mediterranean, or at least a

Figure 3 Posidonia © Florent Beau – Espaces Maritimes.
Communauté de communes du golfe de Saint-Tropez

large section of it, my preferred terrain on the French side is the area off the coast of the Provence-Alpes-Côte d'Azur region (PACA) and around Corsica. In this area I form underwater meadows, and even a veritable submarine forest. We now know that in the past I was used for many different purposes. My favourite is my use as a packaging material for the export of glassware by Venetian merchants. A more prosaic use was as an insulation material for roofs. Sometimes even as a fertilizer, though less effectively, since serious doubts have been expressed concerning my nutritive value. It is said that, in ancient Rome, I was used in the thermal baths for thalassotherapy. My first usage even goes back to Palaeolithic times, when I was used as rudimentary bedding, thanks to my repellent qualities – I keep fleas and bugs at bay.

If there is indeed some misunderstanding about my real nature, it is down to the appearance of my dead leaves, which form banquettes on the beaches. The uninitiated tend to view this as unsightly, and therefore undesirable. The result was that, for a long time, elected officials, beach club managers and local residents would dispose of me or remove me. Serious error – and illegal into the bargain as we shall see. On the contrary, my presence there is in fact a good sign. Acting as an indicator, I am one of the biological elements used to measure the environmental state of bodies of coastal waters in the Mediterranean.

In fact, without wishing to boast, I am quite simply a vital ecosystem for the Mediterranean. A 'miracle ecosystem' as Professor Boudouresque, one of the scientists who has been instrumental in making me better known, likes to call me. In his pioneering research, subsequently confirmed by a number of reputable studies, I am known as the 'richest and most productive population in the whole of the Mediterranean'. It is estimated that I shelter between a fifth and a quarter of its biodiversity – and I also ensure a number of other ecological functions: a species reservoir, a refuge and feeding area for marine fauna, a source of oxygen for the water (I produce more oxygen per equivalent area than the Amazon forest but, like it, I am gradually disappearing . . . you see what I'm driving at), a stabilizer of sediments, a swell absorber, an element of protection for coastlines against coastal erosion (hence my crucial importance in maintaining the beach as a sandy zone). I produce a very large quantity of organic matter and, in my capacity as a carbon sink, my contribution to slowing down global warming is regarded as increasingly valuable. As a result of all this, any damage I sustain inevitably has extremely detrimental effects. My decline results in a reduction of biodiversity (a quantitative and qualitative depletion in terms of species), the exhaustion of fish stocks, the proliferation of invasive species (in particular *Caulerpa taxifolia*, better known under the rather unpleasant nickname of 'killer algae'), a deterioration in the water quality, the acceleration of coastal erosion and therefore shrinking beaches. A study, published in 2015 and covering the entire Mediterranean basin, estimated that over the course of half a century my presence had declined by about one-third overall, arguably with considerable local variation. '*Posidonia oceanica* is the most threatened seagrass habitat: almost half of the surveyed sites in the Mediterranean have suffered net density losses of over 20% in 10 years', according to the First Mediterranean Assessment Report in 2020. At this rhythm, some scientists predict that within the next half-century at best, I shall be practically extinct, at least in certain areas.

The reasons for this situation are multiple, ranging from climate change to the development of urban ports, and including marine pollution caused by intensive farming, even if the respective roles and the interaction between them have not yet been fully identified. One thing is sure, however – the majority of them are the result of human activity, including the practice of wild anchoring; or, in other words, the growing numbers of huge luxury vessels mooring outside sandy zones. Their anchors (weighing several dozen kilos) and chains (several dozen meters) inflict damage on me and, over time, end up destroying me, both at the time of anchoring and when the boat is leaving, but also between the two, thanks to the minimal stabilization movement. It is true that I live for a long time, on a scale of centuries or even millennia, but the rate of growth of my rhizomes is as slow as my capacity for regeneration is feeble. As a result, any prospect of replanting is difficult and can only be envisaged in the long term.

Now, I don't mean to complain, but the wake-up call has been slow to come. Ever since the postwar years at least, I have been destroyed as a result of port developments particularly in urban zones. I am now protected and even triply so, on a national, European and, more broadly, international scale. In France, a ministerial decree dated July 1988 concerning the list of protected marine plant species, not only prohibited my destruction but also prevented anyone from buying and selling me, and from transporting or hawking me, including in a dead or broken-up state. I also feature in a decree dated September 1989, pursuant to the 1986 'Loi Littoral' (a law governing protection of the coastline). Within the European Union (EU), the May 1992 directive, called 'The Habitats Directive', on the conservation of natural habitats and wild fauna and flora, which established Natura 2000, the Europe-wide network, made me a 'natural habitat of Community interest'. As such, I come under European norms in marine matters and in particular am covered by the Marine Strategy Framework Directive adopted in June 2008. More generally, I am protected by texts to which the EU is a signatory alongside other countries – sometimes, in the best case, up to fifty of these. I feature in annexe 1 of the Berne Convention on the Conservation of European Wildlife and Natural Habitats in its amended form, from 1996–7 (it originally dated from 1979), as a protected species, and am covered under annexe II (list of threatened or endangered species) of the Barcelona Convention for the Protection of the Marine Environment and the Coastal Region of the Mediterranean in its 1995 revised form.

Consequently, in the absence of special authorization, damaging me in any way constitutes an offence, defined by the French environmental code (article L.415-3 to be specific) and by the August 2008 law on environmental responsibility, extended by an order in January 2012, covering the conservation of all non-cultivated plant species and natural habitats. This is an offence punishable by administrative and criminal sanctions and, more precisely, by a prison sentence of up to three years and a 150,000-euro fine. It makes you wonder why people fail to think of me when they talk about 'crime'. There are, incidentally, conservation programmes devoted to me. Because I am increasingly regarded as an important issue for local authorities, I am monitored in the context of an agreement called Ramoge (an acronym formed of letters taken from Saint-*Ra*phaël, *Mo*naco and *Ge*noa), which concerns the protection of coastal waters in the Mediterranean. A network of protection and surveillance, called Tempo, was created in 2011, exclusively for me. Research has been carried out on how local communities should manage my presence, with a particular focus on evaluating what is involved in the removal process – who, why, how and at what cost. The French agency for biodiversity (now part of the French Office for Biodiversity) is on the case.

All in all, there are encouraging signs, but they remain ambivalent. In April 2015, the *Direction départementale des territoires et de la mer* (DDTM), acting as a mouthpiece for the Ministry of Ecology, wrote to the mayors of coastal towns in the Var region, reminding them of the rules around beach nourishment (the addition of sand), an implicit sign that the rules in question were not being fully respected. In April 2019, the *Direction régionale de l'environnement de l'aménagement et du logement*, or DREAL (Department of the Environment, Planning and Housing) of the PACA (Provence-Alpes-Côte d'Azur) region, through its 'Biodiversity, Water and Environment department' (and thanks to the discreet help of a private public relations agency), published a leaflet focusing entirely on me, with a view to improving the way local communities managed my presence on the beaches. This sums up the key facts, listing all the reasons why I should be protected, both ecologically and legally, the pressures I face, and how best to take care of me. The general tone is not, however, purely ecological. No risk of any green tyranny here. On the contrary, the message is one of conciliation between ecology and economy. Among professionals, it is what is known as 'integrated management':

> Posidonia, a marine plant found only in the Mediterranean, fulfils multiple ecological roles. The banquettes, formed from the dead leaves of Posidonia, are washed up by the sea onto the beaches and play a major role in eliminating erosion. The cycle of the accumulation and then removal of these banquettes by the sea is part of the natural function of the beach. These banquettes must be preserved. However, an integrated management may sometimes be necessary in order to reconcile the conflicting pressures of the conservation of fragile environments, the need to limit erosion and issues relating to tourism.

Everything hinges on that 'however' – a simple little conjunctive and, somehow or other, the entire landscape changes. Given that the entire regional economy depends on tourism, here I am suddenly being praised for my 'ecosystem services'. That learned-sounding expression is less obviously problematic than that of 'natural capital' for example, yet it needs to be treated with the same amount of suspicion. This is one of the elements driving both my absorption into the economy using a utilitarian and commercial rationale, in other words, my relegation to the status of 'resource'.

Besides, if the 'artificialization of the coastline' is indeed signalled as the primary cause of my 'decline' and if the three examples given – development of the coastal zone, beach nourishment, removal of the banquettes – are indeed relevant, an argument based on a vicious circle, they conveniently draw a veil over the ravages caused by luxury yachts. The same applies to the Mediterranean Strategy for Managing Moorings of Pleasure Boats, drawn up both by the DREAL and the *Préfecture maritime de Méditerranée*. This 'strategy jointly agreed by government departments' specifically identifies the problem. 'If the development of luxury sailing is part of the economic activity of the Mediterranean, an increase in numbers of wild moorings on sensitive sites or on equipment intended for other purposes, could have dramatic consequences', we read. Further on, a special section focuses on 'illegal moorings'. All well and good, *but* . . . 'The strategy applies in particular to boats of less than 25 meters. Given its specificity, a further analysis on large yachts will probably be carried out at a later stage.'

The situation has since been partially rectified. In June 2019, three years after an initial text more tightly regulating the mooring of the largest boats, a decree was issued by the *Préfecture maritime de Méditerranée*, which directly concerned me, this time targeting yachts of all sizes.

Toulon, 3 June 2019
Prefectural decree no. 123/2019
Establishing the general framework for the anchorage and stopping of vessels in the French inland and territorial waters of the Mediterranean.
[. . .]
Considering that the action of anchoring and stopping of French and foreign vessels in the French inland and territorial waters of the Mediterranean are actions under the navigational and public order authority at sea, falling under the competence of the maritime prefect;
[. . .]
Considering the obligations of France with regard to the conservation of good environmental quality of the waters;
Considering the scientific studies transmitted to the maritime prefect showing further degradation of Posidonia meadows

associated with the anchoring of large vessels (beyond 24 meters);

Considering the necessity of regulating the anchoring and stopping of vessels flying the French or foreign flag, in the French inland and territorial waters of the Mediterranean, for the purpose of ensuring the defence of sovereign rights and interests of the Nation, maintaining public order, safeguarding people and property, and protecting the environment;

Considering the necessity of establishing mooring areas compatible with the safety of navigation, State security and the protection of endangered species;

[. . .]

Article 6 – Special Provisions regarding the protection of the marine environment

6.1 Ship anchoring shall not compromise conservation or lead to the destruction, alteration or degradation of habitats of endangered marine plant species.

6.2 It is therefore forbidden to anchor in an area corresponding to a habitat of protected marine plant species where this action is likely to affect it.

[. . .] Article 8 – Prosecution and Punishment

The offences of this decree expose the perpetrators to the prosecutions and punishments provided for in article L.5242-2 of the transport code and articles R.610–5 and 131–13 of the penal code.

There you are, all set out in black and white. All that remains now is for it to be applied . . . The matter is far from settled but, thanks to the competence of vigilant and tenacious professionals, things are starting to change.

Chapter 15

The Marine Observatory

A tricky place to find unless you are familiar with the area. The best way is to locate both the cemetery and the tip – the offices of the Marine Observatory are situated between these two. It is hard not to see this as a sign of a downgrading in status, even if the premises give an impression of being a rather agreeable place to work. In fact, in a region that leans very much to the right of the political spectrum, the organization's scope for action is questioned and its very existence is constantly challenged. Rivalries are played out, first of all on a local scale, between the twelve different administrative districts – some coastal, some inland – which make up the association of local municipalities, and then between the local and the national level, since the Marine Observatory is part of a regional and local authority, while also being responsible for producing charts for the central government. If it has no equivalent elsewhere, a peculiarity that could act as an argument to challenge its existence, it benefits from a long-established presence, which has in fact placed it firmly within the institutional landscape. Initially the result of a constitution process laboriously set in motion in 1993, it officially came into existence during the 2000s.

According to the official description, the Marine Observatory of the gulf of Saint-Tropez district community council is an 'inter-municipal advisory structure of a scientific, technical and educational nature, which aims to support sustainable development through knowledge of coastal environments, awareness-raising among users and the management of coastal environments and their uses'. This wide-ranging mission calls for an extensive range of theoretical and practical skills and its success relies on both solid scientific knowledge (ranging from marine ecology to oceanography and including both physical and human geography) and the diving skills needed to examine the condition of the seabed. It also involves the ability to work both with elected members and with professionals from within the tourist industry, as well as with visiting holidaymakers and sometimes school children, in order to familiarize them with the issues relating to mooring, at sea, and to the sand dunes, on land.

Since 2000, the year in which an *ad hoc* monitoring was set in place, the Marine Observatory has been at the forefront of the conservation of Posidonia or, more accurately, of charting its decline. One decade on, its members reported 'irreversible impacts resulting from human activity on more than eleven hectares of the Posidonia meadows', within a range defined as the '*Corniche Varoise*', classed as a 2000 Natura site. Of the thirty-one different sectors designated by them along the coast and covering four different administrative districts, the level of concern was considered to be 'strong' for six of these, and 'very strong' for two of them: notably the Bay of Briande, on the one hand (very close to a property owned by businessman Vincent Bolloré); and the zone around north Pampelonne, on the other. In the latter case, at least, both the high volume of traffic and the large scale of the vessels were to blame. Everything points to the fact that the first decade of the century was particularly harmful for Posidonia. Since then, the decline seems to have accelerated as a result of an increase in tourist-related boating activities.

An essential stage in the milk run, in any of its variations, this section of the Mediterranean coast is famous for being a key area for the world's luxury yachts. The concentration of vessels is so dense that the Marine Observatory has begun to record their activity using an automatic identification system (AIS). Between 2010 and 2020, up to 300 moored boats at any one time were recorded in the Bay of Pampelonne alone (in other words, approximately one-third more than at the end of the previous decade), including a hundred or so luxury yachts, with an average length of around fifty meters.

The need to respond to the problem of damage caused by the mooring of luxury yachts was triggered by the introduction of management measures in the context of the Natura 2000 initiative. But it is in direct contradiction with the local economy of a luxury coastal resort, reliant on tourism and especially on its identity as a holiday destination. The tension between economy and ecology is particularly acute here. The entire Saint-Tropez peninsula has featured on the list of 'registered sights' since the 1950s and its coastline boasts numerous environmental awards. This area has long been in the sights of the *Conservatoire du littoral* (the coastal protection agency), while at the same time being part of a joint-management scheme with the *Conservatoire d'espaces naturels* (CEN – conservatory of natural spaces), which, since 1992, has been active in conserving the dune belt in particular. The entire *Corniche Varoise* is a protected marine area as a consequence of its association with the Natura 2000 network. It is part of the Port-Cros national park, the borders of which were extended in 2016. In the meantime, the beach operators' association can easily claim to be the largest employer in the region. In fact, the entire local economy, even outside the coastal section, has tended to reconvert to high-end production in order to meet the demands of a clientele made up of wealthy holidaymakers.

The compromise between these divergent interests has a name: ZMEL (*zone de mouillage et d'équipement léger*

– anchorage and light equipment zone). An organized system of collective mooring, adapted to areas defined by a heavy presence of holidaymakers and of significant environmental concern. This represents a middle way, which avoids the twin traps of the large-scale development of port zones, on the one hand and a complete ban, on the other, and instead prioritizes an approach based on regulation through both management and legislation. This involves both the payment of a fee and the introduction of police regulations. Not surprisingly, the process is a long one and deadlines initially announced have already been missed. When an extended study began in 2014, the inauguration was projected for 2018. The deadline was subsequently moved to 2022, and has since been even further delayed, due to legal complications. In the meantime, the Marine Observatory has tried to limit the extent of the damage by pushing for a gradual conversion towards more ecological floating anchorages, even if simply the use of marker buoys. But the battle is far from won and, for the time being, as the number of boats in the area continues to rise, *Posidonia oceanica* is receding.

Chapter 16

At sea/in a meeting

It is a startling sight, especially for someone accustomed to the unobstructed views of the Channel or the Atlantic coast. In high season, looking out to sea from Pampelonne Beach, the marine horizon is densely crowded with vessels of varying lengths. There is a disproportionate presence of very large yachts, from which it is possible to take a speed boat and visit the fashionable beach attractions without the risk of social promiscuity. The employees of the most prominent beach restaurants keep a careful watch for the arrival of these exclusive vessels, with their promise of a coveted clientele, and can list which ones they have or have not already sighted during the season and which ones they hope will soon arrive.

On a similar model to land grabbing (the seizing of land in general or specific areas in particular) academics and activists now talk about 'ocean grabbing', a term used to refer to the largely unwarranted appropriation of maritime zones or marine resources. This concept generally applies to cases of privatization or commercial exploitation, typically in the context of fishery resources, but also for the purposes of conservation. It sometimes involves the eviction of local populations from coastal areas ('coastal grabbing'). In the case in point, the presence of a large quantity of boats does not prevent people from swimming or from enjoying the water and the potential hazards (smells, debris, murky water) are not always noticeable to local people or holidaymakers, perhaps because they have simply got used to them, and it is difficult to accuse the boats or their owners of actually appropriating or closing off the space. Yet there they are, in full view, filling and shaping the landscape with their unmistakable presence.

It was on a much smaller scale that we set off in August to accompany agents from the Marine Observatory on one of their trips out to sea. We had arranged to meet on a small beach little known to tourists and almost deserted as we prepared to depart. We were not, however, embarking on this small motor vessel for pleasure. This trip was part of a patrol undertaken by officials from this public body on a regular, if not systematic basis. For them, it was not just a matter of keeping an eye, as it were, on luxury yachting, or of carrying out compliance checks. Our hosts were involved in an investigation and we were shadowing them in the context of our own research. Often less clear than we would like to admit, the distinction between researchers and those under scrutiny was decidedly hazy in this case. The people we were accompanying and, in a sense, observing, were themselves conducting their own survey, with a bilingual questionnaire and a database at the ready. Theirs had a practical purpose related to the creation of an eco-mooring zone. (Super)yachts have the infuriating habit of not dropping anchor in the sandy zones situated in the south of the bay, but instead dropping it further north in the middle of the Posidonia meadows; in other words, directly opposite the most glamorous restaurants. The intention, therefore, was to encourage captains to opt instead for the sandy seabed, without driving them away altogether with rules or fees they would judge respectively to be too restrictive and too high.

The approach was both gradual and unpredictable. First of all, they needed to spot a boat not yet featuring in the respondents' database, currently numbering around fifty. Once the boat had been alerted and they had made their way towards it, there needed to be someone available. In many cases their calls went unheeded, as though nobody was on board, and we were obliged to go away empty-handed. When someone did deign to put in an appearance in response to the call, there was no guarantee that they would be willing to speak. Sometimes a bodyguard would show his face and indicate that we had better make ourselves scarce. In some cases, in order to facilitate the conversation, a member of the Marine Observatory was invited to board the vessel, on an external gangway but, more often than not, there would be no such invitation and the two of them would end up shouting themselves hoarse, each from their own boat. When communication did successfully take place, everything emphasized our inferior position, starting with the comparatively ludicrous size of our skiff.

The interruption needed to be a brief one. Scepticism often prevailed, accompanied by a rather thinly disguised threat to set a course for a more easy-going destination. There was a shared consensus along the lines of. 'Won't it kill business? There are already fewer and fewer boats. – If you make things too restrictive, people will leave France and go to Croatia. – It will penalize the smaller boats. – If we have to pay 100 to 150 euros, it won't really affect us, but . . . Why pick on this bay? – Set up nature reserves nearby.' 'Intelligent' ecology, yes, one of them sums up, 'obsessive' ecology, no.

One captain, who agreed to engage in a conversation, nevertheless immediately issued a warning: if he saw his clients coming, we would have to interrupt the conversation at once. Clearly, he did not relish the prospect of new restrictions on mooring. He explained that there was a considerable risk that this would simply end up driving boats away. Would people who hire a yacht for several tens or hundreds of thousand euros a week really baulk at paying out 150 euros a day in order to moor in good conditions, including from a security point of view? Yes, really. The man was adamant, his gaze firmly fixed on the shore where his clients might reappear at any moment. As soon as they started to head in our direction, we needed to beat a hasty retreat. This sense of urgency seemed more than simply a matter of not wishing to be disturbed. After the conversation – a brief one lasting barely more than a few minutes – had been interrupted, we exchanged glances, aware that we had all formed the same impression and eager to put a finger on exactly what it meant. All of us agreed – far from the relaxed atmosphere conveyed by advertisements for the sector, the predominant emotion experienced by our interlocutor was fear.

*

In one of the rooms in the community and cultural centre, which had been made available by the municipality, the protagonists had begun to gather, twenty or so people grouped around tables arranged in a big square. The group included various representatives from *le département,* in the form of a delegation representing the sea and the coastal area, *la région* (a French administrative area made up of several *départements*), the city council, the association of local authorities, the Marine Observatory, the beach operators' organization, the agency for protected marine areas, and representatives from the luxury yachting industry. The meeting had been organized in order to explore the prospect – albeit an uncertain one, since much disputed – of creating an eco-mooring zone. More precisely, the concerned parties had been invited to discuss the results of a feasibility study carried out by a specialized private consultancy. The two men representing the consultancy on that occasion expressed a point of view, which, if not neutral, was at least that of outsiders not involved in any immediate local issues and with knowledge of similar situations in other parts of the world, allowing them to bring a comparative and pragmatic perspective to the matter. In other words, they had effectively taken on the role of experts. This key role facilitated the formal cordiality of the discussions, which in turn helped to diffuse any tension arising from conflicting interests. On the surface it was a seemingly balanced approach and evidence of good intentions, which nevertheless only just succeeded in disguising intractable antagonisms.

The document of roughly one hundred and fifty pages submitted for general consideration, the key elements of which were presented orally with the help of slides, was in accordance with this intention. Brimming with charts, graphs and diagrams it set out the issues and options, with the help of figures and pictures, in an attempt to reconcile, or at least consider, the legal, economic and environmental points of view. The French situation appeared to be fragile. Italy and Spain were riding high, increasing their capacity to welcome luxury vessels. The administrative requirements and environmental regulations made it unlikely that new ports for luxury yachts would be built in France, particularly those capable of welcoming the largest vessels, which sometimes have difficulty finding space in the western Mediterranean. Eastern competition – Croatia, Turkey, even Montenegro – was more and more serious with the price–quality ratio becoming increasingly favourable. In France, the number of visiting boats had stagnated over the last two or three years. The risk of a decline of interest in France was all the more serious in that the larger boats tended 'to move in a pack', we were warned – providing grist to the mill of critics of the supposed refinement of what effectively amounts to the herd-instinct. The financial contribution required by an organized mooring system should not be seen as a tax on the right to moor, but rather as a payment for access to a secure zone. It is easier to charge for peace of mind brought about by a reduced risk of collision than for commitment to the environmental cause.

Those representing economic interests spoke out. The 'rich' should not be stigmatized – that was the sort of thing that only happened in France. Nor should it be suggested that yacht owners alone should contribute to environmental conservation, which in fact concerns everyone, in accordance with the liberal strategy of the individualization of responsibilities. Owners were fed up, they said, of being singled out and made to pay. The word 'racket' was pronounced, at least as a spectre to be kept at bay. There were calls to consider the specific nature of the zone in question, to avoid losing sight of the identity of the *Corniche Varoise* in oversimplified comparisons. Those representing public interests, for their part, pointed out that there were laws that needed to be respected. That anchoring on Posidonia is illegal, even if the offence is rarely, or never, sanctioned. Calmly, and in veiled terms, they pointed out that, in the absence of any agreement, there was the risk of a total ban being imposed. An outcome, which, of course, 'nobody' wanted. There was unspoken acquiescence. But the thought was on everyone's mind, nevertheless.

When the meeting came to a close, a polite atmosphere reigned, with, in addition, just a hint of southern warmth. It would be fascinating to know what was said on the walk home or in the car when people could finally speak openly. Probably nobody had learned very much. The opposing forces had come together and drawn up their battle lines. Without abandoning their restraint, the members of the consultancy responsible for the survey had, towards the end of the meeting, confirmed what preliminary investigations had hinted: at the rate things were going, within the next half-century, the beach was in danger of disappearing as a result of erosion.

A proposed legal definition of ecocide describes it as 'any generalized or systematic action included in a list of offences that causes widespread, lasting and serious damage to the natural environment, committed deliberately and in knowledge of this action'. Another definition refers to 'the extensive damage to, destruction of, or loss of ecosystem(s) of a given territory, whether by human agency or by other causes, to such an extent that peaceful enjoyment by the inhabitants of that territory has been or will be severely diminished'. Looked at from any angle, it is difficult to see why either of these definitions should not apply in this case.

Chapter 17

Caught red-handed

'Midnight dumping': this expression refers to the deliberate illegal unloading or dumping of hazardous substances. As the term implies, these acts often take place at night. As common sense might suggest, darkness favours such activities as a result of lower levels of supervision, reduced visibility, less likelihood of being caught. All of this hinders prosecutions and particularly convictions, given that the courts require proof obtained *in situ* by direct observation. The expression also applies however to daylight hours, although it would not occur to anybody to use it in the case on which we are focusing here and, in fact, it is not the same thing. The problem is that this distinction between the letter of the law and the manner in which it is applied implies a clear distinction between what does or does not constitute environmental crime. Yet this activity does indeed amount to an offence against environmental laws, and one which, because it takes place under water, is all but invisible, even in full daylight.

The competent local authorities are well aware of the problem. They concede that, in fact, impunity tends to be the general rule in this matter. This impunity, extending well beyond the case of Posidonia, firstly takes advantage of a statistical contingency, which, however, is by no means an ancillary issue. The system according to which such cases are counted and recorded, even before any valid calculation is made, inevitably conceals the existence of environmental damage, while at the same time claiming to provide an apparent objectivity.

Do you have general statistics about offences against the maritime environment?
- We're in the process of obtaining them because the ministry has just sent us – so it's all very recent – instructions on environmental policing ... however at the moment we're not doing anything ... we'd have to manually go through the data to sort out and look again at which boxes to tick in order to establish what comes under the heading 'marine environment'. Bearing in mind that the issue is not always very clearcut, or at least not to our satisfaction, in terms of what exactly comes under 'marine environment'. If there is an offence in the heart of the park which relates to fishing, do we put it under fishing or do we put it under marine environment, or under them both? Today, it's neither one nor the other. That's why at the moment we don't have a clear monitoring process and why I'm not in a position to be able to give an exact number.
- *And so there are no statistics about how the numbers breakdown between the administrative and the penal? They would need to be worked out?*
- We'd have to work them out, in the knowledge that neither are completely exclusive of the other. On a case-by-case basis, either we take one, or we take the other, depending on what is most practical; it often depends on what period we are in, and then on the efficiency and speed that we want to give to the procedure. We're all too well aware that delays within the penal system and administrative delays are not necessarily the same thing.

Which explains why, at the end of 2016, an official from the DDTM (*Direction départementale des territoires et de la mer* – Department for Land and coastal management) in the Var region, echoed the comments of a representative of the CEN (Conservatoire d'espaces naturels) describing the terms and limitations of the policing powers at his disposal on the terrestrial front. He admitted that he often found himself down-grading certain offences, and simply fining someone for behaviour that should be liable for a penal procedure for reasons that are purely contingent and practical – avoiding an excessively long procedure, and above all making sure that the damage in question has been stopped. Yet, in the case of Posidonia meadows, as in so many others, the way in which the infringement is legally defined and classified is crucial:

> The other curb on our activity, is that currently, in order for something to be regarded as an offence against Posidonia, the offenders have to be caught red-handed. That means we have to catch them in the act . . . Either we have to be able to send divers underwater to check that an anchor is moored in the meadows, or we have to be there at the moment when the anchor is raised and verify that there are still leaves attached to it. Provided of course that the anchor hasn't been slightly shaken as it is raised so that all the leaves have fallen off . . . So, it's quite dif-ficult to be there at the right moment in order to make that check. Today, we have sectors where bans have been organized according to zones; areas where there is Posidonia have been identified and these have been decreed as zones where any mooring is totally banned. We've done the same thing all across the whole *département*, and it all gets complicated very quickly when you realize that Posidonia is virtually everywhere and when you also see that in some of the zones where it is found, it's not evenly established and there are pockets of sand which are not necessarily associated with any destruction . . . where really there is space to put a boat without it affecting the nearby

meadows. That's really the problem we have at the moment in terms of controlling the marine environment. Incidentally, the Civil Code, for any offences, is indeed 'destruction or damage to a protected species'.

So, given that the necessary condition constituting a legal case involves being caught red-handed, a full-scale sea patrol would have to be in place in order to record any relevant evidence. The lack of resources is exacerbated by an objective empirical difficulty making any clampdown very difficult, if not impossible. The presumed scale of this difficulty nevertheless brought a smile to the face of one member of the Marine Observatory:

> It's not the end of the world . . . There's nothing complicated about it. There's a maritime police force, a nautical police force . . . they are divers and if they want to dive down to look at an anchor and see if it is moored on the plant meadow or not, they can. It's not that complicated . . . it can be done. It's simply a matter of taking up position and waiting for a few hours for someone to turn up and then arresting them, and that's something they do all the time. If they really want to, all they have to do is to take up position, wait for the anchor to be raised and then they'll be able to see if there's any damage . . .'

Just as is the case with labour inspections or fiscal obligations, whether from behind a desk or on the high seas, as soon as there is any question of criminal activity among the powerful, the means to do something about it are found to be lacking and obstacles suddenly become insurmountable. (This is not necessarily the case: in 2021, after a long wait, law enforcement officers finally carried out sea patrols in the Mediterranean, resulting in the recording of hundreds of offences.)

But there is something else. This near-impossibility cannot only be attributed to a lack of resources. It can only be fully understood if it is seen in the context of underlying socio-economic power relations. In reality, powerful pressure is indeed exerted by those representing economic interests, from luxury yachting itself but also from beach establishments, without taking into account the support, at least tacit, of local businesses whose livelihoods depend on the holiday resort and on luxury tourism. Publicly, it would be difficult in the current climate for such representatives to dismiss environmental concerns completely. The ecological cause has in fact imposed itself as an obligatory rhetorical device in planning conflicts of this type ever since the beginning of the 1990s. But, in the best-case scenario, that is to say when it is not just a simple rhetorical device, this commitment takes second place to arguments of an economic, or social basis (on the grounds of saving jobs), in order to ensure that discussions go more smoothly.

Yet the resources currently lacking in order to respond to the criminal offence of damage to the Posidonia meadows were once to be found in the very same region. In the 1970s, free camping was popular along the coastline of the Maures region, as photos taken at that time clearly demonstrate. The authorities termed this 'wild' camping and described the situation as alarming and difficult to contain. Because of the damage it caused to the environment it was partially suppressed and partially subject to regulations. As an alternative, camping 'on the farm', further inland, was promoted. And, unlike luxury yachting, the hard-line approach to campers remains unchanged. It will not of course escape anyone's notice that, in the two cases, those involved represent social groups with extremely divergent resources, both materially and symbolically.

Water crimes, maritime crimes, aquatic crimes – these phrases or similar wordings can be found in official documents, produced by legitimate institutions. Something has clearly been identified and labelled as falling within the jurisdiction of crimes and offences associated with the marine environment, and programmes of action have duly been put in place. But, most of the time, to what exactly do these refer? Firstly, to activities clearly catalogued as reprehensible on an international scale, such as illegal overfishing. Secondly, to the dumping of toxic waste in the form of oil spills, with their instant dramatic impact. A far cry from the current case, all the more given that criminal activity can be uncovered in unexpected places, far from the mafia circles or other organized criminal networks that usually capture attention when it comes to 'environmental crime'.

This enormous intellectual and institutional structure, which demarcates, hierarchizes and categorizes the fields of both minor and more serious criminal activity, stigmatizes certain prohibitions, while allowing others to be tolerated and even to thrive, responds with severity towards offences committed by ordinary people and with a certain indulgence to those committed by the powerful and unevenly handing out little arrangements and privileges, corresponds to what Michel Foucault suggested should be named 'the differential supervision of illegalities'. Yesterday, as today, this forms a well-known yet discrete part of the machinery driving class domination.

Chapter 18

When Capitalocene and eco-socialism take to the water . . .

It is incredible what you can end up finding on a superyacht: everything from class struggle to ostentatious wastefulness, from tax avoidance to environmental crimes, from greenwashing to social separatism . . . At first sight, luxury yachting might seem far removed from, and unworthy of, the major debates about the coming of the Anthropocene or the legal recognition of ecocide as an international crime. In reality, it leads us directly to them. In doing so, it provides justification for swapping the figure of the Anthropocene for that of the Capitalocene. In spite of all its faults, the former had at least the merit of substituting the much-hackneyed notion of 'crisis' for that of an irreversible change of epoch. While endorsing this idea, the latter has a more solid sociological and political basis: technological gigantism, squandered energy, climate change, all embodied not by generic humanity but by a very specific, although infinitesimally small, segment of society. Tweak the thread of superyachting and the entire fabric of fossil-industrial capitalism begins to unravel.

And set against that comes eco-socialism, or social ecology as Murray Bookchin pioneeringly called it – but it comes to the same thing here – which, quietly identifies a practical case (a target). Such a stance is based at the very least on a double hypothesis. Recognizing that the environmental question is an integral part of the social one, or, in other words, noticing how social and environmental problems are intertwined, eco-socialism sets out to find a shared solution. What is more, while conscious of the length and complexity of the chains of mediation between the global system and local phenomena, it traces the origin of these problems back to a system rooted in capitalism itself. A system that is, by definition, expansive, even limitless, and which leads to the inseparable duo of productivism and consumerism.

From this perspective, the denunciation, however robust, of the staggering scale of inequalities does not go far enough. Neither does the equally justified condemnation of an oligarchic power less and less convincingly disguised as a democratic organization: a necessary stopping-off point but not the final destination. It is clear that superyachts embody inequalities in the most eloquent and even the most caricatural way possible. And that includes what, at the risk of a semantic confusion, are increasingly referred to as environmental and sometimes ecological inequalities. These involve not only inequalities in terms of exposure to negative factors (pollution, hazards) and inequalities in terms of access to assets (amenities, natural resources), with the attendant effects on health and, more broadly, on wellbeing, but also the impact on particular social groups and the resulting harm this can cause. In other words, the socially differentiated responsibility for the resultant damage. Superyachting provides a perfect illustration of an astonishing sleight of hand: notably the capacity of the wealthiest individuals to exonerate themselves from the social and environmental cost of their activities and behaviours. This is a master-stroke of genius, which transfers this cost onto other social groups, including the poorest, while at the same time individualizing the responsibility thus transferred. It is not just a question of inequality, then, but also of domination.

An eco-socialist reading cannot, however, be satisfied with targeting a fraction of the population, whatever that may be (1%, 0.1%, etc.), even though we are well aware of the mobilizing potential, the power to affect people, that such an approach does entail. This needs to be emphasized all the more emphatically in that the case of superyachts particularly lends itself to being viewed from such an angle, in both qualitative and quantitative terms. On the one hand, these sectors are poorly divided up from a sociological point of view. They give a doubly deceptive impression of the social hierarchy in general and of the dominant class in particular, whose lifestyle is by no means confined to its most ostentatious manifestations. On the other hand, the obsession with figures is just as likely to impede the understanding of the mechanisms that generate inequalities, as it is to stimulate it. 'Correcting the excesses of a small number of people, situated at the very top of the social hierarchy', warns for example, Louis Maurin, 'is a good way of not changing anything at the core of a system which produces inequalities.' At the core of the system lies a web of social relations called capitalism.

Indeed, would it not amount to falling into a trap were we to target inequality, or more broadly, capitalism, albeit from a genuinely critical stance, on the basis of its most flashy, even glaring manifestation? It will come as no surprise now that it is not really superyachts as such that interest us. Let us just say that they provide us with a toehold. A very small one admittedly, but a toehold all the same. After all, we have to start somewhere, get hold of some concrete evidence, especially when time is short. Even if it was simply a thought experiment, designed to fire our imaginations a little? A way of taking at face value the notion that eco-socialism is, in the words of Michael Löwy, 'a project for the future, a horizon of the possible, a radical anticapitalist alternative, but also – and inseparably – an agent of action *hic et nunc*, here and now, around concrete and immediate proposals'.

Superyachts teach us four things about the super-rich, as Nicole Aschoff explained in *Jacobin*: they live in their own world; they are above the ordinary business cycles; they do not care about the planet; they should pay a lot more in taxes. She goes on to conclude:

> Superyachts encapsulate everything wrong with our for-profit system – as billions struggle to survive, and the planet tumbles toward ecological catastrophe, the world's richest people sail away, sheltered from the rough seas of capitalism.
>
> These superyachts, like the billionaire class, shouldn't exist. We need to institute a global wealth tax, shut down tax havens, and, yes, take their boats.

Take their boats, yes, but to do what with them? Simply have them scrapped? Dreaming aloud about a mosaic of 'First revolutionary measures', Éric Hazan and Kamo went one step further than simple requisition, entertaining themselves by imagining the transformation of yachts into sailing schools for school children. Other issues would then arise: enrolment fees (unconditionally free of charge?), managing fuel costs (nationalizing petrol multinationals in order to plan and ration production?), and so on, in never-ending circles. Beyond just the spoils of war, subvert the conditions of possibility of superyachts . . . and of their world.

Describing with humour his fascination at the discovery of a maritime geolocation application, a journalist from *The New York Times* joked that this was 'a tracking device for indefensible wealthy capitalists, and it will probably come in handy when the revolution begins'. Some owners seem to be perfectly aware of all this, though without for the moment displaying undue anxiety. 'I have a joke', guffawed Bill Duker, former business lawyer, disbarred after being convicted of fraud against the US federal government before successfully retraining as a computer specialist and speaking from aboard the yacht *Sybaris*. 'If the rest of the world learns what it's like to live on a yacht like this, they're gonna bring back the guillotine.'

Sources

This book is based on a variety of sources. In this section I list the main ones according to category, before giving additional information for each chapter, working sometimes in order of appearance, sometimes in chronological order – at the risk of a certain (arbitrary) overlap, as material originating from the same source may appear in several chapters.

Academic texts

The most specialized contributions are those by: Geographer Emma Spence: 'Towards a More-than-Sea Geography: Exploring the Relational Geographies of Superrich Mobility between Sea, Superyacht and Shore in the Côte D'Azur', *Area*, 46 (2), 2014: 203–9; 'Unravelling the Politics of Super-rich Mobility: A Study of Crew and Guest on Board Luxury Yachts', *Mobilities*, 9 (3), 2014: 401–13; 'Eye-Spy Wealth: Cultural Capital and "Knowing Luxury" in the Identification of and Engagement with the Superrich', *Annals of Leisure Research*, 19 (3), 2016: 314–28; 'Beyond the City: Exploring the Maritime Geographies of the Super-Rich', in R. Forrest et al. (eds), *Cities and the Super-Rich*, London, New York and Shanghai: Palgrave Macmillan, 2017, pp. 107–25.

Superyachts sometimes get a mention in works focusing more generally on the 'super-rich', e.g.:

Thomas Birtchnell and Javier Caletrío (eds), *Elite Mobilities*, London and New York: Routledge, 2013, *passim*; Iain Hay (ed.), *Geographies of the Super-Rich*, Cheltenham: Edward Elgar, 2013, *passim*; Mike Featherstone, 'The Rich and the Super-Rich: Mobility, Consumption and Luxury Lifestyles', in N. Mathur (ed.), *Consumer Culture, Modernity and Identity*, New Delhi: Sage, 2014, pp. 3–44; Tim Di Muzio, 'The Plutonomy of the 1%: Dominant Ownership and Conspicuous Consumption in the New Gilded Age', *Millennium: Journal of International Studies*, 43 (2), 2015: 492–510; Paula Serafini and Jennifer Smith Maguire, 'Questioning the Super-Rich. Representations, Structures, Experiences', *Cultural Politics*, 15 (1), 2019: 1–14. Last but not least, as part of a much broader ethnographic approach: Ashley Mears, *Very Important People. Status and Beauty in the Global Party Circuit*, Princeton and Oxford: Princeton University Press, 2020, *passim*.

On the subject of environmental damage, see:

Michael Lynch et al., 'Measuring the Ecological Impact of the Wealthy: Excessive Consumption, Ecological Disorganization, Green Crime, and Justice', *Social Currents*, 6 (4), 2019: 377–95. The argument is taken up by Megan Day, 'The Rich Are Committing Crimes Against Nature', *Jacobin*, 17 July 2019. Since the book was published in French, a Twitter account called Yacht CO_2 tracker (https://twitter.com/YachtCO2tracker) has been very active in this respect.

A number of French sources focuses on water sports and sailing or yachting in general. Notably: Nicolas Bernard, *Géographie du nautisme*, Rennes: Presses universitaires de Rennes, 2016; Vincent Herbert, Christophe Gibout (eds), *Plaisance et urbanité*, Villeneuve-d'Ascq: Presses universitaires du Septentrion, 2017).

There are, however, very few academic texts on luxury sailing/yachting, with the exception of Michel Desse and Simon Charrier,

'La Grande Plaisance, un secteur économique en plein essor', *Études caribéennes* [online], 36, 2017.

Grey literature and specialized sources

This generic heading includes work produced by actors within the sector, from constructors to consultants, including commentators. In particular:

+ specialized websites such as: The Superyacht Group, Superyacht Times, Yacht Harbour, YachtCharterFleet, Boat, Superyacht Life, Superyachts.com . . .;
+ Yacht Construction websites, such as Burgess, Feadship or Lürssen (among many others), or specialists in sales and charter like Camper & Nicholsons;
+ websites aimed at the very wealthy, e.g. Wealth-X or Capgemini, or associated with the luxury sector, such as Robb Report, Luxury Launches . . .;
+ geo-localization or auto tracking websites: Marine Traffic and Vessel Finder.

Main documents consulted:

Superyacht Intelligence, *Economic Analysis of the Superyacht Industry*, February 2012; The Wealth-X and Camper & Nicholsons *State of Wealth, Luxury & Yachting Report*, 2016; *The Superyacht Annual Report Wealth*, 2018; Capgemini, *World Wealth Report*, 2018; Wealth-X, *World Ultra Wealth Report*, 2019; Superyacht Times, *The Seatec 2020 Intelligence Report and Monaco Yacht Show*, 2019; Superyacht Times, *Monaco Yacht Show*, 2019; Superyacht Times, *The State of Yachting 2021*, July 2021; . . . as well as several editions of *The Superyacht Report* (hereinafter *TSR*) published between 2017 and 2020. The *Global Order Book* has been published since 1992 by ShowBoats International/Boat International Media.

In French, available official data, in particular those produced by the Department of Infrastructure, Transport and the Sea, under the Ministry of Ecology (*La Plaisance en quelques chiffres*, editions 2006 and 2016), contain almost no information on luxury yachting.

General media

The number of articles has risen sharply in recent years. In the case of some newspapers such as the *Guardian*, *The Financial Times* (including a supplement featuring a section entitled 'Yachts and Marinas') or, in France, *Le Monde*, the subject is part of the specialized area of one or several journalists.

See in particular:

The *Guardian* – Rupert Neate, 'Inside the Billionaires' Superyachts: Helipads, Tennis Courts and a Missile Defence System', 26 January 2014; David Batty, 'Superyachts and Bragging Rights: Why the Super-rich Love Their "Floating Homes"', 9 October 2016; Rupert Neate, 'World's Largest Superyacht: A Floating Private Members' Club for Billionaires', 10 February 2017; Archie Bland, 'Sailing Away: Superyacht Industry Booms During Covid Pandemic', 12 December 2021.

The Financial Times – Jonathan Guthrie, 'Marine Industry: Superyacht Luxury', 10 November 2003; Victor Mallet, 'Haves and Have Yachts', 15 October 2005; Andrew Hill, 'Superyachts Magnify Billionaires' Worst Traits', 8 August 2016; Richard Donkin, 'A Guide on How to Purchase a Superyacht', 28 September 2016.

The New York Times – Patricia Kranz, 'In the World of Superyachts, Bigger Is Better', 16 March 2008; Nazanin Lankarani, 'For Superyachts, the Bigger the Better', 20 September 2011; Shivani Vora, 'When Only a Superyacht Will Do', 22 June 2019; Peter Wilson, 'No One Needs a Superyacht, but They Keep Selling Them', 10 October 2019; Paul Sullivan, 'Yachts Are for More Than Lounging', 6 March 2020; Peter Wilson, 'The Seas as the Ultimate Coronavirus Isolation? Not. So. Fast', 20 April 2020.

Le Monde – Marie-Béatrice Baudet, 'Les Français sont de plus en plus nombreux à naviguer', 1 December 2000; id., 'Mon bateau est plus beau que le tien', 17 September 2008; id., 'La Course au plus gros bateau du monde', 16 August 2011; id., 'Les Nouveaux Atours des milliardaires', 14 August 2019.

In addition, and even above all, see the economic and financial press, specializing on the business world, such as: *Forbes*, e.g.: Tim

Thomas, 'The World's Biggest Yachts and Their Billionaire Owners', 25 March 2012; Alicia Adamczyk, 'How Much Does a Superyacht Really Cost?', 8 April 2015; or, in France, *Les Échos* (e.g. Paul Molga, 'Les Mégayachts de la démesure', 5 July 2016). Here, as below, media references cited are either from print or online versions.

Videos

A considerable number of publicity videos (sometimes unwittingly comical) can be found on the most popular online accommodation websites as well as on the websites of some constructors and specialized media sources. In addition, some reports are available in general interest publications, such as 'Luxury for the Super-Rich', *Deutsche Welle*, January 2020 (featuring the quote from Bill Duker cited in the final chapter).

Notes and references

Preface to the English Edition
References to:
Max Horkheimer, *Dawn & Decline: Notes 1926–1931 and 1950–1969*, New York: The Seabury Press, 1978 (citation p. 76); Gabriel Zucman, 2015, *The Hidden Wealth of Nations. The Scourge of Tax Havens*, Chicago: University of Chicago Press, 2015; Branko Milanović, *Global Inequality. A New Approach for the Age of Globalization*, Cambridge: Harvard University Press, 2016; Aurélien Berlan, *Terre et liberté. La Quête d'autonomie contre le fantasme de délivrance*, Saint-Michel-de-Vax: La Lenteur, 2021; Louis Maurin, *Encore plus! Enquête sur ces privilégiés qui n'en ont jamais assez*, Paris: Plon, 2021; Andreas Malm, *How to Blow Up a Pipeline*, London: Verso, 2021 (citation p. 91); Ilona M. Otto et al., 'Shift the Focus from the Super-Poor to the Super-Rich', *Nature Climate Change*, 9, February 2019: 82–7; Beatriz Barros and Richard Wilk, 'The Outsized Carbon Footprints of the Super-Rich', *Sustainability: Science, Practice and Policy*, 17 (1), 2021: 316–22; Lucas Chancel, 'Global Carbon Inequality over 1990–2019', *Nature Sustainability*, 5, 2022: 931–38; Edouard Morena, *Fin du monde et petits fours. Les Ultrariches face à la crise climatique*, Paris: La Découverte, 2023.

Chapter 1. A colossus at anchor

Observations carried out in February 2020. References to:

Stéphen Liégeard, *La Côte d'Azur*, Paris: Quantin, 1887; Guy de Maupassant, *Sur l'eau*, Paris: Gallimard, 1993 [1888]; Emma Goldman, *Living my Life*, London: Penguin, 2006 [1931]; *see also*: Etienne Juillard, 'La Côte des Maures. Son évolution économique et sociale depuis cent ans, étudiée dans la région de Saint-Tropez', *Revue de géographie alpine*, 45 (2), 1957: 289–350; Gilbert Buti, *Les Chemins de la mer. Un petit port méditerranéen: Saint-Tropez (XVII–XVIIIe siècles)*, Rennes: Presses universitaires de Rennes, 2010, p. 32.

Chapter 2. One form of excess can conceal another

References to:

Richard Horton, 'Offline: Being Relaxed about Yachts', *The Lancet*, 376, 16 October 2010; George Hughes, 'The Self, Signification and the Super-Yacht', *Leisure Studies*, 12 (4), 1993: 253–65; Mike Davis and Daniel Monk (eds), *Evil Paradises: Dreamworlds of Neoliberalism*, London and New York: The New Press, 2007; Mike Davis, 'Fear and Money in Dubai', *New Left Review*, 41, September/October 2006: 47–68 and *Planet of the Slums*, London and New York: Verso, 2006, pp. 12 and 93; Oxfam, *Public Good or Private Wealth?*, January 2019, p. 12.

Citations:

Tony Paterson, 'Yachts with Champagne Showers Tempt the World's Super-Rich to Germany', *Independent*, 3 February 2011; Marie-Béatrice Baudet, 'Palaces sur les flots', *Le Monde*, 17 August 2019; David Harvey, *The Enigma of Capital and the Crisis of Capitalism*, Oxford: Oxford University Press, 2010, p. 110.

Chapter 3. Floating palaces

Information taken from:

Patricia Comant, 'Grande plaisance: la course au luxe', *Les Échos*, 30 November 2007; Patrice Piquard, 'Le Yacht, ultime babiole de la *dolce vita*', *Capital.fr*, 19 January 2012; Hugo Cox, 'Super-size my Superyacht: The Quest for Bigger Boats and Gadgets', *Financial Times*, 20 October 2016; Mark Abernethy, 'Superyachts Show Size Matters to the Super Rich', *Financial Review*, 21 June 2019; Tyler Rogoway, 'You Can Buy Paul Allen's Octopus, Arguably the World's Most Incredible Yacht', *The Drive*, 8 September 2019; James C. Young, 'Super-Yacht' Era here with New Astor Craft', *New York Times*, 23 September 1928.

References to:
Michel Pinçon and Monique Pinçon-Charlot, *Les Ghettos du gotha. Au cœur de la grande bourgeoisie*, Paris: Le Seuil, 2007, ch. 5; Luc Boltanski, Ève Chiapello, *The New Spirit of Capitalism*, London and New York: Verso, 2005, pp. 361–71; Bruno Cousin, Sébastien Chauvin, 'Is there a global super-bourgeoisie?', *Sociology Compass*, e12883, 2021: 1–15; La Découverte, 2017, pp. 197–205; Henri Lefebvre, *Writings on Cities*, Oxford: Blackwell, 1996, pp. 158–9; Max Weber is cited by Norbert Elias, *The Court Society*, Oxford: Blackwell, 1983, pp. 37–8.

Chapter 4. Specimens
Information taken from ship construction and yacht charter websites.
'*A*' features in numerous (French) press articles, e.g.:
Gerard Lebailly, 'Un méga yacht de milliardaire russe en escale', *Ouest-France*, 24 September 2016; Marilyn Mower, 'Solandge: The 85m Superyacht Designed for Pure Enjoyment', *Boat International*, 16 January 2015; Philip Lee Harvey, 'Float Your Boat', *Daily Telegraph*, 14 March 2015.

Chapter 5. UHNWI
Information taken from the documents of Camper & Nicholsons, Wealth-X and Capgemini mentioned above.
References to:
John Kampfner, *The Rich. From Slaves to Super Yachts, A 2000–Year History*, London: Little Brown, 2014; *see also*: 'From

Ancient Castles to Mega-Yachts: What History Teaches us About the Super-Rich', *Guardian*, 14 October 2014; *see also*: Jonathan Beaverstock and Iain Hay, 'They've "Never Had it so Good": The Rise and Rise of the Super-Rich and Wealth Inequality', *Handbook on Wealth and the Super-Rich*, Cheltenham: Edward Elgar, 2016, pp. 1–17.

Citations:
Rory Jackson, 'The Superyacht Industry Manifesto', *TSR*, February 2020, p. 3; Rupert Neate, 'Life and Death on a Superyacht', *Guardian*, 26 May 2018.

Chapter 6. Yachting lifestyle
Information taken from:
Nick Jeffery, 'Cruising the Côte d'Azur', *Yachting*, 199 (3), March 2006: 102–6; Victoria Craw, 'Young Workers Tell Us What it's Really Like Working on Super Yachts Overseas', *News.com.au*, 27 May 2014; Dana Kennedy, 'Debauchery, Danger and the Dirty Secrets Aboard the Super-Rich's Superyachts', *Hollywood Reporter*, 12 May 2015; Anoosh Chakelian, 'Lost on the Outlaw Seas', *New Statesman*, 18–24 September 2015; John O'Ceallaigh, 'Inside the Secret World of the Superyacht Elite', *Daily Telegraph*, 1 February 2017; Rupert Neate, 'Life and Death on a Superyacht', *Guardian*, 26 May 2018; Tom Mullen, 'Why Purchasing a Superyacht is about Acquiring a Lifestyle', *Forbes*, 18 September 2019; Hillary Hoffower, '9 Things Superyacht Crew Members Wish They Could Tell Their Billionaire Guests – but Won't', *Business Insider*, 23 September 2019; Nick Waymark, 'The Very Real Risks Behind Superyacht Glamour', Aegis London, 4 June 2018; M. Agnew, 'Inside the Sordid World of Superyachts', *Marie Claire*, 3 April 2020.

References to:
Benoît Collombat and David Servenay (eds), *Histoire secrète du patronat de 1945 à nos jours*, Paris: Arte/La Découverte,

2014 [2009]: 620–1; Alizée Delpierre, 'The Price of "Golden" Exploitation: How Money Flows from the Super-Rich to Domestic Workers Support Inequalities', *Socio-Economic Review*, 20 (4), 2022: 1539–1566.

Chapter 7. The 'abode of production'

Information taken from:

Adam Fiander, 'MYBA Economic Impact Study Concludes Revenue Growth and Job Creation are Key Aspects of Superyacht Industry', *Broad Reach Communications*, 12 March 2013; Daniel Shea, 'MYBA: Economic Impact of Yachting', *Onboard Online*, 21 March 2014; Anon., *Yachting Matters and The Yacht Owner*, 27, 2014: 133; *see also*: Don Hoyt Gorman, 'Luxury Vessels Prove Their Worth', *Financial Times*, 24 September 2013; Katie Warren, 'I Got into a Monaco Yacht Show Gala for VIP Super-Yacht Buyers and Industry Elite . . .', *Business Insider*, 30 September 2019; The 'Hidden Abode Of Production': Karl Marx, *Capital. Volume 1*, New York: Dover Publications, 2011, p. 123.

Chapter 8. Amsterdam's Red Party

Information taken from documents from The Superyacht Group.

Citations:

'The Superyacht Forum – An Event Worth Attending', 2017, p. 27; ICOMIA, 'Giving the Industry a Voice: Environmental Rules', in *The Superyacht Report*, 166, 2015: 85–8.

Chapter 9. ISF-IFI & Co.

Information taken from:

Laurent Mauduit, 'Yacht de luxe, 800.000 €/sem., à louer, s'adress. à Bernard Tapie', *Mediapart*, 22 January 2012; Ingrid Feuerstein, 'Réforme de l'ISF: le flop de la taxe sur les yachts', *LesEchos.fr*, 18 July 2018; Thomas Chemel, 'Réforme de l'ISF: la "taxe yacht" rapporte des clopinettes', *Capital.fr*, 19 July 2018; Jean-Victor Semeraro, 'La Taxe sur les yachts fait pschitt!', *Capital.fr*, 25 July 2019; Benoît Floc'h, 'Taxe sur les yachts: histoire d'un naufrage fiscal', *Le Monde*, 8–9 September 2019; Guillaume Guichard, 'Les Taxes sur les yachts et les voitures de luxe rapportent très peu', *Le Figaro*, 27–8 July 2019; Aurélie Lebelle and Matthieu Pelloli, 'Qui a coulé la taxe yacht?', *Aujourd'hui en France*, 26 September 2019; Les Décodeurs, 'Comment Malte est devenue une place forte de l'optimisation fiscale', *Le Monde*, 8 November 2017; Jean-Baptiste Chastand, 'Les Stratégies des riches Français pour payer moins de taxes sur leurs yachts', *LeMonde.fr*, 8 November 2017; Yann Philippin, 'Voyage fiscal à Malte, paradis des yachts', *Mediapart*, 8 November 2017.

More generally:

Élise Barthet, Audrey Tonnelier, 'Les Riches, grands gagnants des premières mesures de Macron, selon l'OFCE', *Le Monde*, 15 January 2018; Audrey Tonnelier, 'Les Ultrariches, grands gagnants de la fiscalité Macron', *Le Monde*, 13 October 2018; Romaric Godin, 'La Très Politique évaluation de la réforme de l'ISF', *Mediapart*, 2 October 2019; Audrey Tonnelier, 'Avec la politique économique de Macron, "les 5% de Français les plus pauvres devraient voir leur niveau de vie se réduire"', *Le Monde*, 5 February 2020; Romaric Godin, 'Emmanuel Macron reste un "Robin des bois à l'envers"', *Mediapart*, 5 February 2020.

References to:

Pierre Madec, Mathieu Plane, Raul Sampognaro, 'Budget 2018: pas d'austérité mais des inégalités', *OFCE Working Paper*, Sciences Po, 01, 2018; Michel Pinçon and Monique Pinçon-Charlot, *Le Président des ultra-riches*, Paris: Zones/La Découverte, 2019, chs. 2 and 10; Alexis Spire and Katia Weidenfeld, *L'Impunité fiscale*, Paris: La Découverte, 2015; Bruno Amable, Stefano Palombarini, *L'Illusion du bloc bourgeois*, Paris: Raisons d'agir, 2018 [re-ed.], pp. 178ff; Philippe Steiner, *Les Rémunérations Obscènes. Le Scandale des hauts revenus en France*, Paris: La Découverte, 2011; ATTAC et Fondation Copernic, *L'Imposture Macron. Un business model au service des puissants*, Paris: LLL, 2018 (citations p. 27 and p. 106).

Chapter 10. Riding the (financial) storm

References to:

Michel Desse and Simon Charrier, 'La Grande Plaisance, un secteur économique en plein essor', article cited, and to the following reports, *The State of Wealth, Luxury and Yachting*, op. cit. and UBS/PwC, *Riding the Storm. Market turbulence accelerates diverging fortunes*, 2020.

Citations:

Giles Whittell, 'The Superyacht Survival Story', *Boat International*, '101 Biggest Yachts in the World. Plus: "The Business of Yachting"', January 2019; Martin Redmayne, 'A Darwinian Moment. The Evolution of Superyachting', *Superyacht News*, April 2020; Evan Osnos, 'The Haves and the Have-Yachts', *The New Yorker*, 18 July 2022. Data for the graph obtained from: Superyacht Times, 'The State of Yachting 2021', July 2021, p. 26.

Information taken from:

Terry Macalister and Kirsty Scott, 'Superyachts Turn Tide for Industry', *Guardian*, 31 December 2003; Sophie Péters, 'Le Nautisme tient bon la barre', *La Tribune du week-end*, 10 September 2010; Jamie Dunkley, 'Superyacht Owners Turn to Arson to Get through Austerity', *Daily Telegraph*, 9 April 2012; Andrew Trotman, 'Superyacht Firms Feel more Buoyant after Growth and Orders Pick Up', *Daily Telegraph*, 25 September 2013; Richard Donkin, 'Top Yards Thrive, Smaller Ones Struggle to Stay Afloat', *FT Special Reports*, 'Yachts & Marinas', 23 September 2015; id., 'Industry Endures a Crucial Year/Crucial Year for Industry on the Lookout for Signs of Confidence', *Financial Times*, 25 September 2013; Anon., 'Record Number of Superyachts Being Built since the Financial Crisis', *Boatinternational.com*, 14 December 2015; Rebecca Taylor, 'Supply and Demand', *Superyacht Intelligence, Annual Report 2015*: 29–30; Polly Mosendz, 'The Ultra Rich Bought Bigger, more Expensive Yachts in 2015', Bloomberg.com, 4 March 2016; Simon Greaves, 'Wave of Demand Buoys Superyacht Sales',

Financial Times, 19 April 2016; Doug Gollan, 'The Superyacht Industry is Poised for Growth', *Forbes.com*, 13 April 2016; Kalyeena Makortoff, 'Brexit Boost for Superyacht Industry as Sales Rise above Sinking Pound', *The Independent*, 27 September 2016; Rory Jackson, 'The Superyacht Industry Manifesto', *TSR*, February 2020: 1–7.

Chapter 11. Conspicuous seclusion

The idea of conspicuous seclusion is taken from an article I wrote with Isabelle Bruno: '"Before Long There Will Be Nothing but Billionaires!" The Power of Elites over Space on the Saint-Tropez Peninsula', *Socio-Economic Review*, 16 (2), 2018: 435–58.

References to:

Thorstein Veblen, *The Theory of the Leisure Class: An Economic Study of Institutions*, New York: The Modern Library/Random House, 1961, p. 29; Alice Le Goff, *Introduction à Thorstein Veblen*, Paris: La Découverte, 2019, p. 64 *sq.*; Erving Goffman, *Asylums: Essays on the Social Situation of Mental Patients and Other Inmates*, New Brunswick and London: Aldine Transaction, 2009; Jonathan Friedman, 'The Relocation of the Social and the Retrenchment of the Elites', *Social Analysis*, 48 (3), 2004: 162–8; Bryan Turner, 'The Enclave Society: Towards a Sociology of Immobility', *European Journal of Social Theory*, 10 (2), 2007: 287–303; Michel Foucault, 'Of Other Spaces', *Diacritics*, 16 (1), 1986: 27 (thanks to Giulia Mensitieri for reminding me of this section).

Information taken from:

Jack Kelly, 'The Rich are Riding out the Coronavirus Pandemic very Differently than the Rest of Us', *Forbes.com*, 1 April 2020; Emma Reynolds, 'How the Wealthy Are Preparing for the Next Pandemic, from Investing in Private Travel and Superyachts to Building Underground Bunkers', *Business Insider*, 3 July 2020; Brendan Greeley, 'A Superyacht is a Terrible Asset', *Financial Times*, 26 March 2022.

Chapter 12. The political geography of luxury sailing

Reference to:

Marcus Rediker, *Villains of All Nations: Atlantic Pirates in the Golden Age*, New York: Verso, 2012.

Information taken from:

Marie Camière, 'Le Superyacht, une industrie *made in* Italy', *Industrie & technologie*, 1 December 2008; Rhona Wells, 'Super Yachts. The Ultimate Toy', *Middle East*, October 2009: 62–3; Anon., 'MCA Chief Underlines the Importance of Superyacht Industry', *States News Service*, 29 September 2014; Emma Gorman, 'Britain's Superyacht Success Story', *Management Today*, 44, February 2015; William Mathieson, 'New Luxury Destinations Aim to Win Affections of the Super Rich', *Financial Times*, 28 September 2016; Louise Shannon, 'Superyacht Tax is Costing Jobs', *Whitsunday Times*, 14 June 2018; Henry Druce, 'Heliski by Day, Spend the Night in a Superyacht – Is This the Ultimate Luxury Holiday?', *Daily Telegraph*, 25 July 2018; Catherine Sabino, 'Inside the Hot Mediterranean Harbors Where Billionaire Yachts Compete to Stay', *Forbes.com*, 2 August 2018; Arabella Youens, 'Cruise Control', *Country Life International*, 22 May 2019; Rory Jackson, 'Monaco and the Côte d'Azur: Are They the Global Superyacht Capitals?', *Superyacht Report*, 197, September 2019; Hubert Vialatte, 'Sète veut attirer les méga-yachts en centre-ville', *Les Échos*, 20 February 2018.

Chapter 13. Playing the eco-friendly card (greenwashing)

Information taken from:

Anon., 'Green Mega-Yachts: Not-so-Filthy Rich', *The Economist*, 950, 30 April 2011; Risa Merl, 'Does the Eco-Friendly Superyacht Exist?', *Boat International*, 4 February 2015; Romain Clergeat, '"Nature", le super-yacht le plus dingue du monde', *Paris Match*, 13 March 2018; Chris Museler, 'The Greening of Superyachts', *New York Times*, 2 September 2016; Rowena Marella-Daw, 'Turning the Tide: The Sustainable Future of Superyachts', *Luxury London*, 25 June 2019.

Citations:

Jean-Louis Fabiani, 'Rural, environnement, sociologie', in P. Hamman (ed.), *Ruralité, nature et environnement*, Toulouse: Erès, 2017, p. 116; Michael Lynch et al., 'Measuring the Ecological Impact of the Wealthy . . .', art. cited, p. 390.

Chapter 14. Posidonia

Website for GIS Posidonie: https://gisposidonie. osupytheas.fr. *See also* the short documentary made by Andromède Océanologie: 'L'impact des ancres sur les herbiers de posidonie' (June 2019), available online.

Information taken from:

Charles-François Boudouresque and Alexandre Meinesz, *Découverte de l'herbier de posidonie*, Parc national de Port-Cros/ Parc naturel régional de la Corse/GIS Posidonie, cahier 4, 1982; Charles-François Boudouresque et al., *Préservation et conservation des herbiers à Posidonia oceanica*, Ramoge Pub. 1–202, 2006 (in particular p. 161 *sq*.); *see also* in English: Lecture by Charles-François Boudouresque: 'At the crossroads of the past, current problems and the future of the Mediterranean: The Posidonia meadow, a miracle ecosystemet, https://labexmed.hypotheses.org /8864; CSIL/ CREOCEAN, *Bilan de la gestion des banquettes de posidonie en région Provence-Alpes-Côte-d'Azur*. PACA region/DREAL PACA/ADEME, December 2011; DREAL PACA, *Améliorer la gestion de la posidonie sur les plages*, April 2019 (citation p. 1); *Stratégie méditerranéenne de gestion des mouillages des navires de plaisance*, DREAL PACA – Préfecture maritime de la Méditerranée – CETE Méditerranée, September 2010; *see also*: 'Impact du mouillage des grands navires en Méditerranée française', *Cahier de surveillance Medtrix*, 6, April 2019.

References to:

Patrice Francour et al., 'Effects of Boat Anchoring in Posidonia Oceanica Seagrass Beds in the Port-Cros National Park', *Aquatic*

Conservation, 9 (4), 1999: 391–400; Josep Lloret et al., 'Impacts of Recreational Boating on the Marine Environment of Cap de Creus (Mediterranean Sea)', *Ocean and Coastal Management*, 51, 2008: 749–54; Luca Telesca et al., 'Seagrass Meadows (*Posidonia oceanica*) Distribution and Trajectories of Change', *Scientific Reports*, 5, 12505, 2015; MedECC, *Climate and Environmental Change in the Mediterranean Basin – Current Situation and Risks for the Future. First Mediterranean Assessment Report*, Union for the Mediterranean, Plan Bleu, UNEP/MAP, Marseille, 2020 (citation p. 356); Virginie Maris, *La Part Sauvage du monde*, Paris: Le Seuil, 2018, pp. 149–52. Translation of Arrêté préfectoral found on: http/onboardonline.com/assets/translation-ECPY-New Anchorage-Regulations.pdf

Chapter 15. The Marine Observatory

See The Marine Observatory website: www.observatoire-marin.com.

Information taken from:

Étude préalable à l'élaboration d'un schéma directeur du mouillage sur le littoral des Maures, December 2011; *Le Mouillage en baie de Pampelonne*, 2013; *Pampelonne à la recherche d'un équilibre. Vers des mouillages sécurisés, confortables et écologiques*, 2016.

More generally:

Mathilde Lordonné, *Bilan de santé du littoral des Maures 2011*, Observatoire marin/Sivom du littoral des Maures; *Charte Natura 2000 – site FR 9301324 'Corniche varoise'*, Préfecture maritime Méditerranée/ Préfecture du Var, July 2013.

Chapter 16. At sea/in a meeting

Observations carried out in August 2015 and September 2016.

References to:

Laurent Neyret, 'Pour la reconnaissance du crime d'écocide', *Revue juridique de l'environnement*, 39 (HS-01), 2014: 177–93 (citation p. 189); Polly Higgins, Damien Short, Nigel South, 'Protecting the

Planet: a Proposal for a Law of Ecocide', *Crime, Law, and Social Change*, 59, 2013: 251–66 (citation p. 257).

Chapter 17. Caught red-handed

Interviews conducted in November 2016 and February 2020.

References to:

Hilary Sigman, 'Midnight Dumping: Public Policies and Illegal Disposal of Used Oil', RAND *Journal of Economics*, 29 (1), 1998: 157–78; Claudette Lafaye, Laurent Thévenot, 'Une justification écologique? Conflits dans l'aménagement de la nature', *Revue française de sociologie*, 34 (4), 1993: 495–524; Michel Foucault, *Discipline and Punish: the Birth of the Prison*, New York: Vintage Books, ch. 4, pt. 2, p. 282.

Chapter 18. When Capitalocene and eco-socialism take to the water . . .

References to:

Andreas Malm, *L'Anthropocène contre l'histoire. Le Réchauffement Climatique à l'ère du capital*, Paris: La Fabrique, 2017; Murray Bookchin, 'Toward an Ecological Society', *Philosophica*, 13, 1974: 73–85; Louis Maurin, 'Qui sont les privilégiés en France?', *Observatoire des inégalités*, 11 February 2019; Michael Löwy, *Ecosocialism: A Radical Alternative to Capitalist Catastrophe*, Chicago: Haymarket Books, 2015, pp. vii–xv; Nicole Aschoff, 'Superyachts and the Super Rich', *Jacobin*, 22 February 2020; Razmig Keucheyan, *Nature is a Battlefield: Towards a Political Ecology*, Cambridge/Malden: Polity, 2016; Éric Hazan, Kamo, *Premières mesures révolutionnaires*, Paris: La Fabrique, 2013, p. 89.

See also (not to mention a considerable body of publications in English on environmental justice): Hervé Kempf, *How the Rich Are Destroying the Earth*, White River Junction, Chelsea Green Pub., 2007, ch. 3; Cyria Emelianoff, 'La Problématique des inégalités écologiques: un nouveau paysage conceptuel', *Écologie & Politique*, 35, 2008: 19–31; Marianne Chaumel, Stéphane La Branche, 'Inégalités écologiques: vers quelle définition?', *Espace, population, sociétés,* 1, 2008: 101–10; Catherine Larrère (ed.), *Les Inégalités Environnementales,* Paris: PUF, 2017.

Citation from James D. Walsh, 'Letter of Recommendation: Yacht Spotting', *New York Times Magazine,* 14 August 2018.